Dedicated to Tarot Readers everywhere, to my fans, and as always to my family and friends who support my writing career.

ISBN: 1491200340
ISBN-13: 978-1491200346

365
Tarot Activities

Deanna Anderson

HOW TO USE THIS BOOK

Despite having 365 activities this book is not necessarily meant to be used every single day of the year, nor does it need to be done in the order listed in the book.

I recommend reading the book, perhaps making a little notation next to activities, prompts, or readings that sound appealing or interesting, and when it is finished cover to cover go back and do the ones you want.

Not all of the prompts are sequential in that they are not organized as far as "you must learn or do this before moving onto this."

I wrote this book simply because there have been times in my life I have wanted to do something—*anything*—with my Tarot cards but not necessarily a reading.

When I was first studying Tarot I learned early on that taking one card and studying it per day is not the most productive way to learn so I started writing down different ideas for how I was going to learn the Tarot, such as "choose a card at random and write down my interpretation."

Eventually, I compiled all of those ideas for this title.

So why 365 and not a different number? When I was in college

I was taking courses in child care and for one of our assignments we were given a blank yearly calendar. We had to come up with 365 activities, one for each day of the year, and none of them could repeat.

The idea was to stretch our imagination and creativity. Try it sometime, come up with 365 of your favorite songs, movies you have seen, plants or animal names, or even cooking recipes.

This book will try to encompass all types of Tarot decks, or cartomancy, so that anyone can use the activities regardless of what type of deck they own.

However, anytime there is a description of a Tarot card it will be based on a Rider-Waite deck and that deck is in the forefront of my mind as I write this book because it is the most common and one many Tarot readers are familiar with. Many other decks that classify them as Tarot are based on the Rider-Waite system as well.

I have also included entries, prompts and activities for Oracle decks (also known as medicine, angel, and power cards) as these tend to not have suits, a Major or a Minor Arcana.

The entries in this book are meant to be used as by:

1) groups
2) individuals
3) for classroom instructions
4) to promote discussions/lessons on message boards
5) for the beginners, and
6) for the experienced.

The entries can be used in a variety of ways as well:

1) for journal or group discussion prompts

2) to promote discussions on message boards

3) for class or group assignments,

4) group activities

This book is meant to be enjoyed and to help create not only an appreciation for Tarot and an easier way to learn the craft but also to give people a greater depth of the cards and other ways to interact with them other then just for readings.

It also provides practice with the cards and increases one's confidence in reading them or using their intuition.

Initially, the greater purpose of this book is to build that confidence so Readers can interpret the cards without reading information straight out of a book. I personally feel that while it is okay to check in a book or personal journal for help in reading a card, I think the greatest shame a Tarot Reader can do is to never feel the confidence in reading cards without reading straight from a book.

The worst readings I ever got were from people who only looked up the card in the book and read exactly what it said without trying to interpret it to fit with the positions of the spread or my question and without using any of the elemental or numerical correspondences.

Is a person comes to you for a reading and all you do is read from the book, then why are they coming to you at all? They can buy their own deck and read the guidebook themselves. We, as readers, not only for others but also for ourselves need to gain the confidence to read from intuition and cues in the cards, and not reading from a book. And that is why I created this title; to help gain that confidence as well as provide ideas for lesson plans or group activities for those studying Tarot, and to just add in some fun ways to connect with your cards even when you are not doing a reading.

In the back of this book you will also find a glossary of terms, and appendixes for universal correspondences to the elements, numbers, colors, and symbols.

I have not included interpretations, key words, or key phrases for the cards themselves as everyone using this book might be working with different decks or Oracle cards and the card meaning's will vary from deck to deck.

AN INTRODUCTION TO TAROT

There are literally thousands of different Tarot decks in existence with more being created even as I write this. There is no end to the decks that can be collected from rare and antique to ones based on popular culture.

For whatever interests a person has there is probably a Tarot deck out there that matches. There are also other decks of cards that are referred to as power cards, oracle cards, fortune-telling decks, fortune cards, angel cards, medicine cards, etc.

Tarot cards typically follow the style of what is commonly known as Rider-Waite decks (sometimes seen as Rider-Waite-Smith or RWS) which is named for its original creators, A.E. Waite (mystic and creator behind the cards) and Pamela Coleman-Smith (artist) as well as the Rider publishing company.

Neither Tarot nor the suits or the idea of a Major and Minor Arcana were not invented by Rider-Waite, as it is believed Tarot cards came to us as early as the 14th century; however, Rider-Waite-Smith were really the first to get Tarot into the mainstream and mass-produced.

The Rider-Waite decks are the most popular in the English-speaking world, whereas the Tarot de Marseilles is the most popular deck in Latin countries.

RWS decks have four suits: pentacles, cups, wands, and swords which include the "Pips," or the numbered cards 1-10. There are also four court cards in those suits: Pages, Knights, Queens, and Kings. These pip and court cards make up the Minor Arcana.

There is another "suit" (for lack of a better word) of cards known as the trumps, triumphs, or Major Arcana. These are numbered 0 through 21 and are seen as a spiritual journey.

These cards are archetypal personas or concepts such as the Emperor and Empress (people) or The Moon and the Sun (objects) or Judgment and Strength (concepts).

Tarot decks based on RWS cards will follow a similar pattern, with slight variations.

For example, there is a vampire deck in which cups (water) are depicted as holy water, swords are daggers, and wands are wooden stakes, etc. The suits often vary in decks as well such as pentacles becoming diamonds, discs, or coins and the courts may change from Knight and Page to Prince and Princess.

The Major Arcana might also change such as a High Priest replacing the Hierophant. But, regardless of the changes if a deck is divided into four suits with a Major Arcana it is based on the Rider-Waite system. Typically these decks also have seventy-eight cards although this is not a steadfast rule either.

There are also other types fortune-telling cards, often referred to as oracle cards, that while they are used for divination they are not set up the same as Rider-Waite decks, often with a fewer (sometimes even greater) number of cards and no suits or Major Arcana.

I have a Goddess Tarot deck that is thirty-two cards all depicting a different goddess. Steven D. Farmer is known for creating animal cards, sometimes known as medicine cards that depict different animals.

Neither format of fortune-telling is better than the other, it is all based on individual needs and likes.

Using cards for divination is known as *cartomancy* and we seek the knowledge from the cards for advice, meditation or fortune-telling.

However, keep in mind that the cards may not always be specific, they may not even answer the question in mind as sometimes the intuition picks up a different problem that needs a resolution, and the future they portend is not set in stone.

I always say Tarot gives advice and likely scenarios rather than actually telling the future.

For example, if someone asks "will I be happy if I marry Joe?" the cards might show a lively, love-filled, and happy married life. But when Joe proposes if I say no and marry Tom instead then the future is not equal to what the cards indicated.

Using the cards are not a hard and fast science, we are still learning their secrets and all the ways in which they can be used. Anything in the realm of paranormal, supernatural, or occult are still mysterious and up for speculation, conspiracy, and theories as science has not proven any of these areas (yet). But, there is a long history in everything occult and Tarot cards are no exception.

When I first started this book I had a chapter devoted to the

History of Tarot, but the more I researched the more confusing it got.

Bottom line: the origin of Tarot is steeped in mystery, speculation and theories. We do know that the earliest recorded form of Tarot cards in usage is the 1400's in Italy, and that Tarot was used both as a game and a source of divination.

Which purpose came first is up for speculation and there are those who believe that Tarot as divination came first and then branched off into playing decks, others believe the opposite. There are also theories that Tarot has been around longer than the 1400's.

What we do know is that in Victorian England fortune-telling cards, séances, and other occult practices became popular as parlor games and instead of gathering for tea or horse-races, people gathered to delve into the worlds of the paranormal and supernatural.

With the publication of the Rider-Waite decks, Tarot cards became main stream and thousands of decks are published each year.

For some they have become invaluable tools in their professional, spiritual, and personal lives.

TOP 20 TAROT MYTHS

It seems like everything comes with a myth these days and Tarot is no exception. With Urban Legends, rumors and myths being passed so readily via the internet these days it is no wonder that something as old, as versatile, and as 'mysterious' as Tarot has its fair share of myths, many of which have often kept people away from picking up a deck of cards.

There were several myths that have been in my "general consciousness" ever since I was first introduced to Tarot in my college days, almost twenty years ago, but I also did a quick internet search to see what other myths were floating around out there so that I could address them.

I have come up with twenty of the most common Tarot myths and tried my best to explain why they are not so and to provide a little insight so that others can be put at ease or judge for themselves the validity (or invalidity) of such myths.

Myth #1—"You can't buy your first Tarot deck."

Tell that to all the writers, illustrators and publishers of Tarot decks who depend on you to buy their decks. One of the reasons this is a myth is because there is no basis for why you can't, in fact

Tarot readers encourage it. The idea may have come from a time when it was difficult to buy your own simply because they were not mass-produced and you might only get a Tarot deck by having it handed down from someone.

The 'can't' in the myth was probably more of "can't because decks aren't readily available" and not in the sense that "you can't because it causes cosmic chaos."

Having someone buy you a deck leaves you out of the joy of picking your own or run the risk of getting a deck you don't like, and therefore don't connect with. How likely are you to connect and be able to read a Star Trek themed deck when you don't like Star Trek and don't know a thing about it?

Choosing a deck is, for Tarot readers, one of the great joys in life. It is rather like choosing which book to buy: First you look at the box, then a few cards if you can, you read the description on the back of the deck, and maybe you recognize the author and have other decks of theirs.

Buying your own will not diminish the power of the cards because the power comes from within you. No cosmic hiccups or mishaps will occur because you bought a deck, or bought more than one.

Buying a deck will only cause your wallet to be a little lighter and make you fall in love with Tarot. Another hazard of not buying your own is waiting around for someone to buy you one. Don't wait around, go online or to your local chain bookstore and buy your first (or 101st Tarot deck).

Myth #2—"Place a new deck under your pillow before using it."

This is such a common myth and often one that 'newbies' are told to do, almost as if it is a must and the cards will never be understood if this step isn't completed. Hogwash!

When I first was told this myth my initial thought was "wouldn't that ruin the deck?" The way I sleep the cards would be scattered all over, bent, and probably a few missing.

My second thought was "how does this help me connect to Tarot?" I am not a believer of osmosis in that I can place a textbook under my pillow and wake up knowing all the information within.

That being said, I will not understand Tarot or be able to read cards by sleeping with them. Learning the cards comes by working with and studying them.

The other idea behind this myth is that this helps bond the cards to you, but again I say that working with them and studying them is what bonds you to the cards, not tucking them under a pillow.

If this is a practice you want to employ, by all means there is no harm in it, but it is not mandatory and in my opinion not recommended for fear of damaging the cards.

Myth #3—"Tarot cards are portals to other worlds."

This myth holds no merit because, in short, Tarot cards are pieces of paper with pretty pictures on them. That is not to diminish their value of importance in guiding, aiding, assisting, and communicating with us as readers but it is to say that they are no more portals than the art on the walls of a gallery.

In fact, if anything, the art in a gallery has more energy then a Tarot card in that it was created by hand by an artist. The original art in a Tarot card may have been created painstakingly by hand but at some point it was photocopied, scanned, reprinted and mass-produced.

Anything that is mass-produced I find impossible to believe is a portal of any kind. Granted, we do add our own energies to a deck when we use them but it is not an energy that can open portals.

Myth # 4—"Tarot cards don't work."

They do work, if you have an open mind and believe that they work. Do people believe in prayer? In miracles? If so, then why not Tarot? Aside from people not *wanting* to believe in it for religious reasons (Biblical texts often forbid divination), many people just don't believe in certain things.

Tarot enthusiasts will never convince some people that Tarot works just as some people can't be convinced that prayer works, or that aliens are real.

But, if you are interested in Tarot then believe it works. Keep in mind, a Tarot reading is only as good as the reader. Math works, but if I am bad at math then my equations won't work.

Tarot is the same, and that is why people read books, join discussion groups, or study Tarot on their own. Some have a natural knack for it and can pick up any deck and do a reading having never seen the deck before.

Others have to work with the cards and study them more in

order to be able to read them.

Just as in 'real life' some of us seem to have a born talent for science or math. So, if you study the cards, trust your intuition, and practice then Tarot works.

Myth #5—"You can't read for yourself."

I have no idea where this myth comes from and it appears that Tarot is the only divination form that claims it cannot be performed on one's self. Which is a ridiculous notion; there is no cosmic reason why a person can't read for themselves.

The only problems that can occur when doing self-readings may be a lack of objectivity or it becoming an obsession.

Never use Tarot to decide every action in life, and never replace common sense or seeking medical, psychological, or legal advice.

I am reminded of an episode on the teen TV show "iCarly" where Spencer used a Magic 8-Ball™ (it was a magic meatball in the episode, but the same type of toy) to decide his every decision and after asking several options for what to drink he ended up with ketchup because it was the only thing the meatball said yes to.

Don't use Tarot, or any divination source, this way.

Lack of objectivity comes when a person wants the cards to say a particular thing, so we twist the meanings until it fits with what we want.

However, I have never had this problem and good readers can read for themselves with a certain lack of objectivity. In fact, I find I am harsher on myself than on others because I tend to want to give people positive readings whereas on myself, I already know what is right or wrong and what could happen if I stay on a particular path, I am just looking to Tarot for confirmation.

Otherwise, when I do readings it is without a question in mind so I can remain completely objective as I have no particular outcome I am seeking.

There is also a general belief among some readers that a person should not receive more than one reading per week; again, no cosmic or karmic reason why this is so.

However, asking the same question repeatedly will muddle the answers and leave a person confused just as seeking advice on the same topic from several different friends can leave a person confused.

But, there is nothing wrong with doing a reading every day; in fact, there are some people who draw one card every single day as a glimpse at what the day will hold.

Myth #6— "Tarot will cause the events to happen/cause death."

Tarot cards don't create the future; they only foretell it or give advice for it. Any path that a person is on can be changed depending on the choices a person makes. They are cards, plain and simple, and cannot cause events to happen.

Tarot cards are advice-givers not instigators. Other common myths that tie into this one are that they cards predict death and that they cast spells on people (both of which are addressed in this section).

As I have said before, the cards are pieces of paper with pretty pictures on them. They have no energy of their own until a person uses them. They cannot do anything on their own and even when being read it's the *people* who are interpreting the esoteric symbols and pictograms, the cards are just laying there doing nothing.

The magic, the energy, and the interpretation are in the person.

Myth #7—*"The cards can predict death."*

I don't know of any reader who believes this. The cards are not that certain and even though there is a "Death" card it means transformation or the end of one thing and the beginning of another, not literal death. The cards just don't work that way.

Granted, a reader could interpret a card or reading that way but I would advise against that. No one really wants to know when their own death is coming.

The cards may indicate that a person who is imbibing in self-destructive behaviors may cause health related problems, or that a particularly destructive path may cause problems mentally, emotionally or physically based on their actions or choices but it is not necessarily predicting death (or causing a death).

The cards will never say "you will die tomorrow at noon in a car crash" or cause the events to happen.

Myth #8—*"Tarot / The Devil card / the Death card are evil."*

People have more misgivings about the Devil and Death cards then any other cards in the deck. Read any guidebook or book on

Tarot and they will say the devil is (to put it brief) self-imposed retributions or restrictions and death is transformation or change.

Again, they are pieces of paper with pretty pictures and when mass-produced there is no personal energy, good or otherwise, on the cards. The energy and intent of the cards come from the one who handles them the most.

These coincide with another myth that all of Tarot is evil or has evil spirits attached to the cards and will corrupt those who use it. This belief tends to come from Biblical quotes in which divination is condemned.

Tarot is no worse and no better than any other form of divination so if one does not believe in the evil of divination or the evil of art on a gallery wall then why is Tarot considered evil?

Myth #9—"Never let anyone else touch your cards."

This is actually up to each individual reader and there is some merit to not letting other's touch your cards, but it is an option and not requirement.

Many people believe in the transference of energy and that every object we touch holds some of our energy, especially items that we use often or have personal meaning for us.

Letting others touch your Tarot deck can transfer some of their energy, which can aid in the reading as the reader can often pick up on the querant's energy. But, some readers do not want the energy of other people on their cards. All of this is a personal choice and left up to the reader, not the querant.

Personally, I do let querant's touch the cards as I have them draw a card in a one-card read or they cut the deck. Their own instincts are telling them where to cut or which card to draw.

A good solution is to have two decks: one for personal readings and one for reading for others; this eliminates the problem of having someone else's energy on your cards when you go to read for yourself.

But cards can also be cleansed so if you sense someone's energy on the cards long after they have left, simply cleanse them so they are a "blank slate" for the next read.

Myth #10—"You have to be psychic to read the cards."

Do you have to be psychic to use your own intuition or follow a gut feeling? That's what Tarot is; readers are simply interpreting the cards based on intuition and symbols or signs seen in the cards and their position in the layout.

A person does not need to be psychic to follow or give advice. In fact, based on any of the theories of how Tarot works (which will be discussed in a later section) Tarot doesn't need psychic gifts at all.

Tarot readers are no more psychic then someone answering letters in an advice column, however psychics can use Tarot cards.

Myth #11—"Tarot is difficult to learn."

It is no more difficult to learn then any other subject of study. Anyone can learn to read Tarot just as anyone can learn to knit, to weave baskets, to do math, or to read.

It is a skill that can be learned, sharpened, and honed to perfection. It does take dedication and commitment to learn, but anyone can do it.

Myth #12—"Reading Tarot is dabbling in the occult/witchcraft or you have to be a witch to read them."

Some Tarot readers are witches, but not all witches (or Pagans) read Tarot cards. As for the occult reference, that is purely a subjective term. Some people view it as an occult tool and some people also view occult as "evil".

But, while occult has many definitions (of which one is related to witchcraft, magic, or supernatural phenomena) occult also means "secret or known only to the initiated."

Tarot is about self-initiation (self-learning) and, yes, it is secretive and mystical but it is not evil. Occult practices and witchcraft are also not evil, people are evil—not things.

There are some people that will never be convinced that Tarot and other occult, Pagan, divination, or alternative spiritual practices are not evil and often that battle isn't worth fighting individually.

If you truly believe Tarot is evil you would not have bought this book.

Myth #13—"Tarot cards must be stored in a special manner."

There will be a chapter in this book on how to consecrate or cleanse a deck of cards as some people do believe that energies attract to them. However, these are optional. The cards will work regardless of how they are consecrated, cleansed, stored or handled.

The only complications from storage and handling would be damaged cards but whether you keep them in a box, a black velvet cloth, the original box, or a plastic container is simply a personal or spiritual decision.

There is no "proof" one way or the other that cards need to be stored in a specific place with certain stones or herbs in order to work.

But, if you want them in black velvet wrapped up with a leaf of sage or whether you leave them in the original box tossed in your tote bag with old receipts and candy wrappers the meanings of the cards won't change.

If you are a person sensitive to energies you may want to take special care so that when touching the cards you are not picking up on energies of others and skewing your interpretation of the cards.

Also, if you care for your cards as a precious item and don't want bent corners or scuff marks you may want to take extra precaution handling and storing, but all of these are personal choices.

Myth # 14—"It is bad if a card is upside down in a reading."

I am guilty of this one. I used to think that reversals denoted negative meanings and upright were positive; therefore it was essential to have reversed cards in a Tarot deck.

I quickly learned that within a deck of all upright cards that while there are some cards thought of as more positive or more negative, all of the cards have both positive and negative meanings depending on the question, the interpretation, and its position in the layout or spread.

Take the Sun and the Tower for example. Sun denotes happy, blissful times and the Tower is major upheaval or catastrophe. But, we can also read them in another manner.

In a Past-Present-Future spread the Sun in the past could denote the good times are long gone, but the Tower card in the same position could indicate that the horrible and tragic times are in the past and a person can move forward to happier times.

Myth #15—"Tarot is a Scam."

Sure, there are scam artists out there in all fields and there are probably those who set up Tarot as a business and don't really care about the field itself or know what they are doing.

I heard a story once where a reader told the customer that they had an evil entity attached to them and that for an additional $1500 she'd remove it. Yikes!

I tell people to look at Tarot Readers as anything else, if the price doesn't mesh with what you are willing to pay then don't pay it. It's like buying a car; an old clunker car that doesn't run is not going to be worth a hundred-thousand dollars.

Readings shouldn't break the bank but there is no set standard for what should be charged so customers might see fees based on minute increments (such as $10 for 10 minutes) or a flat fee, if you want to pay it then it is not a scam.

If you are not happy with the reading, do not go back to that person just like you wouldn't go back to a masseuse who was not good. And, adversely, as a reader: always give good readings and don't rip someone off.

Myth # 16—"You have to use reversals."

As stated in myth #14: there is a mix of negative and positive cards in a deck and each card can be either positive or negative depending on the interpretation. Don't ever let anyone tell you that you have to use reversals, this is up to the individual reader and not what others, including the querant, want you to do.

Myth #17—"The Tarot can be used to cast spells or affect other people."

Tarot cards can be used in spells to show intent, for example if I want to make friends I might do a spell with the Three of Cups.

And, it is possible to cast spells on people using the Tarot cards to show intent, although most religious or spiritual paths advise against this for ethical, moral and karmic reasons.

But, the Tarot on its own does nothing. It will not cast a spell or affect a person through a reading or just sitting on a shelf.

Myth #18—"It is dangerous to have too many Tarot readings."

As stated earlier, it can confuse a person if they ask the same question repeatedly in multiple readings. But, there is no danger in doing more than one reading on yourself or others.

People who feel and interact with energy a lot, such as empaths, may need to rest in between readings to recharge their energy, but there is no danger in getting readings or getting more than one.

Myth #19—"You have to use a specific shuffle ritual for the cards to 'work'."

Another silly idea that people tend to have, the cards (in my opinion) are read based on intuition which cannot be affected by shuffling of the cards no more than the outcome of a poker game will be affected by shuffling.

People often have preferred methods, but not a one of them is better or worse than another.

Even if the cards are the result of divine intervention or the cosmic consciousness, the method of shuffling will not matter, whatever message is meant to be given will be given.

The only thing that affects a reading in this manner is if you "stack the deck," that is, to put the cards in a certain order so you can guarantee which cards are coming up.

Myth #20—"You shouldn't use Tarot to play games"

I know some people who think it is an insult to use Tarot in a game such as solitaire or other card games. If you think this then that is fine but on a cosmic level I don't see how this is going to affect the cards.

Again, the cards are based on intuition so how is a game of solitaire yesterday going to affect what the cards tell me today? Some necklaces are used as pendulums and this doesn't affect the swing and sway of it or the answers it gives.

The only adverse effect of using the cards in a game is the wear and tear that occurs. It is not diminishing any cognitive, intuitive, or interpretive powers the cards release in us.

In fact, using them in games can help one learn the meanings of cards and to connect or impart their energy on them. The section on *Group Activities* in this book has several games that can be used with the cards.

BUYING A NEW DECK

Whether it is the 1st or your 101st buying a new Tarot deck is always an exciting time. Readers are always curious to get the deck opened and start exploring it or begin using it.

A connection with a deck is the most important piece of the Tarot puzzle. Being comfortable with it and knowing it well will help readers be able to give a good reading for themselves or others.

I placed this section first in that perhaps some people picking up this book have yet to buy their first deck. If so, then buying a deck should actually be your first activity.

For those of us with several decks, use this section when purchasing a new deck to help familiarize your self with it; this section is good for any type of deck (Tarot or Oracle).

Decks can be purchased at most chain book stores or at metaphysical, Pagan, or New Age stores. However, for anyone without access local stores search online at Amazon, EBay, or Azure Green as well as many other online venues.

Make sure you do some shopping around and don't purchase the first deck you come across. In order to be able to effectively read the cards a person needs to feel a connection with the deck and the images therein.

Some online shopping sites might post pictures of the cards in the decks and Aeclectic Tarot has deck reviews, pictures, and forums where you can discuss decks.

Most websites will not post every picture for copyright reasons. But, if you find a deck you like then do a search and find out more information about it and view some card images.

Also, know if you are getting a good deal or not. Paying hundreds for a Rider Waite deck printed last year is not a good deal but paying hundreds for a deck printed in the late 1800's that is from a limited stock and out of print might be a good deal.

If you are really unsure, ask around on Tarotholics Anonymous (a group on Facebook) or the Aeclectic Tarot forum and experts in the field will help you. Tarot collecting has become as real as collecting rare books, paintings, or antique furniture.

Also check to see if the deck you are buying online is new or used. Most reputable sellers on Amazon or EBay will list whether there is any damage or missing cards to a used deck and if there is any misrepresentation and the seller won't cooperate then the main offices of both sites can be contacted for assistance.

In stores it can be difficult to peruse a deck as they are sealed in cellophane and often store owners will not let customers open a deck to look at the cards, especially in chain bookstores.

Ask shop owners if they have a copy of the deck behind the counter that you can look at. If not, and if you are very unsure of the deck I suggest writing the name down and then looking it up later.

Once you have your first deck or another new one, go ahead and try some of the following activities to get to know your deck better and before actually trying any readings with it. Practice readings will come later.

First Impressions

In a journal or as a group discussion discuss what prompted you to buy this deck as well as your overall impression of the deck (before actually using it to any degree). This can be done in a group or classroom setting with each person bringing in a deck, sort of like a Tarot Show-n-Tell.

Theme of the Deck

In a journal or as a group discussion discuss what the overall theme of the deck (goddesses, animals, crystals, baseball, etc) and how it's represented in the deck.

Think about the following questions: is the theme workable (meaning that it works with Tarot)? How are the elements depicted differently? How does it compare or contrast to other decks? What are the difference in names for the Courts and Major Arcana?

The Feel of a New Deck

When a deck is first purchased I like to sift through all the cards to see each of the depictions, I also like shuffling them to see how easy they are to manage (or not).

Sit down with the deck and look through each of the cards without necessarily trying to interpret (though words or phrases may pop in your head) and just look at each card. By doing this you are getting familiar with the images and your brain is already forming correlations and interpretations. You are also adding your own energy to a deck.

Next, sit with your new deck and shuffle it several times (to me shuffling cards is a very Zen experience). Cards should always be shuffled prior to a reading anyway as most decks are in order in the box.

If you are wanting to use reversals then add those in by cutting the deck several times and each time it is cut flip the stacks around. Another method for adding reversals is spreading the deck over a flat surface and spreading them all around, then straighten into a deck without flipping reversed cards.

Take Notes

Now is the time to take notes on little nuances or notable things about the deck or each card. Don't describe each card in detail, just jot down things that jump out at you or stick out in your mind.

For example, many people don't notice in Rider Waite decks the man in the Seven of Wands is wearing a shoe and boot. Why might this be? Does this mean he doesn't care about appearances? Or perhaps he was in a hurry to defend his territory and just grabbed the first two shoes he found.

Maybe he is one of those flighty people who are never prepared. Paying attention to little things such as these can really give a deeper meaning to cards.

Compare and Contrast

Compare the new deck to others in your collection (if you only have one deck come back to this activity later or look up photos of other decks on the internet) and make a list of similarities or differences.

For example, are the suits depicted differently or the cards given different names, etc? If this is done as a group activity then compare and contrast decks the members have brought.

Three 'Likable' Cards

With a new deck, sort through all the cards without reading the meanings and pull out three that you are really drawn to for whatever reasons: it makes you happy, bright colors, a fun picture, etc. Write or discuss why you picked those cards.

Then, go back and read the interpretations of the cards as given in the accompanying book and write or discuss if you think the interpretations fits your idea of the card or if you still like those cards afterwards.

Three 'Unlikable' Cards

With the same new deck, sort through all the cards without reading the meanings and pull out three that you really don't like, that you seem to have an aversion to. Maybe it's got dark imagery or looks morbid.

Write or discuss why you picked those cards and then go back and read the interpretations in the accompanying book and write and see if they fit with your idea of the card, then write or discuss whether your opinion has changed based on the interpretation given.

Read the Interpretations

Of course eventually you will want to read the accompanying book and see what it has to say about the card's meanings. As you do so, sift through the deck pulling out the corresponding card and thoroughly look at it, comparing what you see to what the author has written about the card.

Write or discuss whether you think it fits or if there is a meaning you'd give that is different.

Side-by-Side Interpretations

Grab at least two decks you currently own and pull out three to five cards from each deck that are similar such as all the Three of Pentacles or all the World cards and do a comparison of interpretations.

For example, is the Page referred to as a Princess in a different deck and does it have a different meaning or message? Take note of the similarities or differences.

This is also a great group activity and each person can bring one deck, then in turn each member of the group pulls out their version of the card and comparisons can be made.

For readers buying their very first deck, come back to this question after you have bought a 2nd deck or look up a specific card in books or the internet that have different images and compare/

contrast using those.

Problem Cards

Whether you have been studying Tarot for a long time or just started, there are likely to be cards that always give you "Tarot Reader's Block" when they come up in a reading (for me it is the Court Cards).

Anytime you stumble on a card whose meaning is difficult for you to interpret, or if you know your problem cards already, write them down and then write why you think you have trouble with these cards (perhaps the meaning hits a sore spot with you, such as indicating divorce) and how you can overcome this blockage.

You can also try writing your own interpretation, key words, or key phrases for this card to help you remember it better.

Try the Deck Out

If this is your first deck and you are not comfortable doing readings yet you can always come back to this activity, and for those more experienced try a basic reading and ask yourself these questions: is the book or guide's interpretation useful? Is it easy to read the cards? Do the cards work in different layouts or different positions?

CONSECRATING & CLEANSING CARDS

Consecrating and cleansing a deck is quite often the same thing and the same methods can be applied, however, they have different definitions. To consecrate something means that you are making it sacred; you are making it "your own" and dedicating it to a specific purpose.

To consecrate a deck you should state its purpose, such as for meditation, divination, or spell work. You also should prepare yourself and a sacred space in which to perform the consecration. Additionally, you can add tools (elemental tools, gemstones, etc) and ask a deity of choice (preferably one of divination) to bless the deck.

Cleansing a deck means you are clearing it of unwanted residual energies, whether they are positive or negative. Cleansing a deck can be done in between every reading or as needed and can be as simple as wrapping the deck in a special cloth or placing it in a pouch or box, or it can complex and ritualized.

Some Tarot Readers will place gemstones in the pouch or box as an aid for cleansing or physic intuitiveness. Crystals are excellent for cleanings, hematite for grounding, amethyst or malachite for psychic powers.

Other methods for cleansing or consecrating a deck might

include:

1) letting each of the elements touch the cards
2) placing the cards on an altar for a twenty-four hour period
3) placing the cards in a windowsill for a twenty-four hour period to can catch sunlight and moonlight
4) reciting a blessing over the cards.

I have included two methods here for cleansing and consecrating and you can choose to follow them or skip to the entry on writing your own. Here are a few different blessings or verses you can also use while either consecrating or cleansing a deck:

Version 1

I bless this deck for evermore to help me open Psyche's door,
show me the answers that I seek, as into the future I take a peek

Version 2

May the cards guide my way, and bless me each and every day

Version 3

Let these cards act as my guide, my intent always be true,
as this advice is given from me to you

Version 4

In the name of (deity of choice), I hereby bless this deck.
May it give me the guidance and advice that I seek.

Consecrating Method 1

Gather two yellow or gold candles, a cloth, essential or fragrance oil, incense, and Tarot or Oracle deck of choice.

Set the candles up on a table or flat surface and light them.

Light the incense.

Lay the cloth down on the table and place a drop or two of oil on it.

Shuffle the cards several times, letting yourself think about what you want the cards to do and allowing yourself to fall into a mild meditative state.

If you have already looked at the cards prior to this then picture a few of the cards you remember seeing.

Think positive thoughts and feel your energy going through your hands and into the cards.

Set the cards facedown in the center of the cloth making sure the light of the candles flickers on it.

Pick up the incense and waft it over the deck.

Lay your hands palms down over the deck and recite a blessing of choice.

Cut the deck once, pick the top three cards and lay them face up.

Write down their interpretations or meanings they hold for you.

Put the cards back, extinguish the candles and incense, and store the cards in your preferred method.

Consecrating Method 2

Gather a candle in each of the colors of the elements (blue, white, green, yellow); also gather and athame (fire), wand (air), bowl of water, and bowl of salt.

On a table or flat surface set up the four candles as such: green (for earth), white (air), orange (fire) and blue (water) in a line on a flat surface leaving space between you and the candles for the next step.

Set the other items up within arm's reach.

Below the line of candles fan out the cards. Light the candles starting from left to right.

Then, in the order given, perform these steps: pick up the salt and sprinkle it on the cards; pick up the wand and touch it to the cards; pick up the athame and touch it to the cards; dip fingers in water and flick droplets on the cards.

As each element you perform each step above recite "by element of _____ I consecrate this deck".

Finally, recite one final, short blessing that dedicates the deck to a purpose or deity.

Put the cards back into a deck, extinguish the candles from right to left and put everything away.

Cleansing Method 1

Gather incense or a feather, a candle in a holder, water, and salt.

Set up the elements on a table or altar with earth (salt) in the north, incense or feather in east (air), water in west, and the candle in south (fire).

Fan the cards out in the center of the elements and starting with north grab a pinch of salt and sprinkle on the cards, then wave the incense or feather over the deck, next pass the candle over the deck so its light shines on it, then dip your fingers in water and flick on the deck.

Hold a deck in the palm of your hand and recite "I cleanse this deck of all energies but my own." Inhale as deep a breath as possible and exhaling slowly, breath on the cards.

Other Cleansing Methods

There are several other quick methods for cleansing or consecrating cards that either require no prep work or take only a few minutes to perform:

Place the deck in a black or white cloth for twenty-four hours (white is a color of purity and black will absorb negative energies). Set the deck on an altar for twenty-four hours.

Place the deck in windowsill for twenty-four hours so it can absorb sunlight and moonlight.

Hold the deck firmly in one hand and slam an edge down hard on a table or hard surface or set the deck down and strike it with a wooden spoon or wand to knock out the energies. The concept here is that it will knock the energies off of it.

Place the deck in a bag or box with gemstones, amulets, talismans or other sacred objects.

Write a Verse or Chant

Sometimes called blessings, charms, verses, chants or words of power, what is said over the cards can be as meaningful as what is being done to them.

Verses or blessings can also be said prior to performing a reading for yourself or for others, as an ending or closure to a reading, or as a way to just bless or cleanse a deck to bond it to you.

The words you create can also be used in conjunction with the actions of consecrating (making sacred) a deck. Whether the verse rhymes or not is a personal choice although rhyming is easier to remember and some practices state that rhyming helps to seal a spell.

Write Your Own Method—Cleansing

Write your own detailed method for cleansing a deck of energies after each use when reading for someone else.

Consider the following questions:

1) are you going to cleanse a deck after every reading or just readings with high energy?

2) are you going to have a separate method for cleansing a deck then for consecrating a new one?

3) what actions, methods, or tools are needed for your cleansing?

4) are you going to use a verse or words of power to be spoken while performing the cleansing?

Write Your Own Method—Consecrating a New Deck

Write your own detailed method for consecrating or empowering a new deck.

Consider the following questions:

1) what actions, methods, or tools are needed for your consecrating?

2) are you going to consecrate a deck only when it is new, on specific days or are your going to consecrate it only when your bond or energies seem to be fading.

3) are you going to use a verse or words of power to be spoken while performing the consecration?

Storing Your Deck

This might seem insignificant, but some Tarot enthusiasts take great pride and thought in how they are going to store their decks.

Some prefer simply to keep them in the box they came in but others wrap them in cloth or store them in wooden or decorated cardboard boxes.

For a Tarot cloth, I recommend getting a bandana; they are the perfect size, are usually a dollar or two, come in a wide variety of colors and designs, and are already hemmed on the sides.

At Pagan or New Age stores there are also wooden boxes that fit Tarot cards and often have sigils or words painted or engraved on them.

There are also cardboard boxes at craft stores that can be decorated with decoupage or paint.

A drop or two of essential oil on a cloth or in the box will further consecrate it and the cards it holds.

ELEMENTAL CORRESPONDENCES

In most Tarot systems the Minor Arcana are divided into suits, as discussed earlier, and while each suit's symbols may vary from deck to deck the elements are basically the same: earth, air, fire, water.

These are the four basic elements or 'archai' as seen in philosophy when ancient philosophers tried to break down the universe into just four concepts.

In science these same concepts become solid (earth), liquid (water), gas (air), and plasma (fire).

These elements have also made their way into Neo-Pagan, New Age and Pagan practices as a basis for magic, spells, and rituals.

In rituals their symbolic creatures (knows as elementals) are called upon to act as guardians to the circle and protect the people inside. In spell work and on altar all four of these things may be present as a way to either guard the user or to aid in the spell.

In Tarot they have specific correspondences indicating a meaning of the card, or what "realm" or area of life the card signifies.

For example, Pentacles are an earth realm and deal with everything that is tangible, worldly and materialistic, the physical realm, whereas the other suits correspond to intangible aspects such as the emotional realm, intellectual realm, and spiritual realm. Knowing the element's correspondences aids a person in reading the Tarot cards.

By knowing the keywords, the numerical correspondence and the element a person can read a card without knowing anything else about the deck or card. Add into that the images and scenes depicted on the card and we have a good reading.

As stated earlier, each element deals with a specific realm of life. This is important to know because as soon as we see the card we immediately know what area of life it is about without actually having read any other part of the card.

For example, if I see a card of cups (or equivalent) I automatically know its water and that means emotions, creativity, womb, or birth. If I see a lot of water cards it may mean that emotions are playing largely in the querant's life or that the situation is one of mixed or high emotions.

Earth is the physical realm and deals with all things that are tangible or our basic needs (jobs, material possessions, money); Fire is the intellectual and communicative realms; Water is the emotional realm; and Air is the spiritual or our internal realms (instinct, personal energy, etc).

Becoming familiar with the suits in Tarot is a valuable asset that will give any reader and a more concise and clear meaning of not only the cards but also what they mean in a reading.

There is an appendix at the back of this book for the correspondences on the basic elements as I know and see them based on a slightly Wiccan background. But, different religions, cultures, and people may have their own ideas of what the correspondences are and there are several good books on the market discussing the elements including my own "Magick for The Elemental Witch."

For these entries use whatever elemental correspondences you are comfortable with. If not familiar with the elements at all then I suggest using the ones in the appendix to keep you on track, but defining your own ideas as well.

For example, in Wiccan and a few other Pagan practices wands are seen as fire (they direct energy) and knives are air (athames are ceremonial knives that are not used to cut anything).

However, my own personal belief is that knives are fire as they are forged in fire and wands are air because I tend to think of them being waved around like a conductor's baton or a stage magician's wand.

Universal versus Personal Correspondence

Based on the elemental correspondences in the back of this book or based on your personal beliefs does the deck you are working with seem to accurately depict the elements? If no, how is it different?

Suit & Element Depictions

What are the suit or elemental distinctions and how are they represented in the deck? For example, if it is a vampire themed deck is the wand now a stake and the chalice a bottle holy water, etc.?

Elemental/Suit Trades & Positions in Life

The suits in both Tarot and Poker decks are said to depict the four major pillars of economy as seen in the Middle Ages.

Swords/Spades represent the military and are soldiers, fighters or heroes.

Pentacles/Diamonds are the merchant trade and can be those who travel to make money.

Wands/Clubs are the agricultural level and seen as farmers or skilled laborers (blacksmith, craftsmen, etc.).

Chalices/Hearts represent the church is anyone of clergy or a religious leader.

What do you think this says about a reading or how can this apply to a reading? If its easer, do a reading for this exercise and describe how the suits trades figure into the interpretation.

Elemental/Suit Trades—Modern Meanings

The trades/positions in life given to the suits are based on more archaic positions. Given what you know about the elements and what they mean think about what modern positions or careers you would apply to the different suits.

Perhaps with pentacles representing business owners and fire representing those in protective services such as policemen or firemen.

Elemental Realms—Key Words

It is generally accepted that the elements each depict a different area of life. Pentacles are the physical realm; cups are the emotional; wands are the spiritual; and swords are the intellectual.

Take each one of these aspects and write key words for each of the elements. For example, what do you think of when you hear the phrase "physical realm?" The key words you write can be based on universal meanings, or can be your own correspondences, or a combination of both.

Keep in mind, you can consider the Major Arcana a fifth element of Spirit and can write key words for it as well.

Elemental Realms—Key Phrases

Using the above key words, write a key phrase that identifies the basic meaning of each element such as "pentacles: focuses on the physical realm of health, wealth, and materialism." Don't forget to include the Major Arcana and write a key phrase for it as the element of Spirit as well.

Alternate Elemental Meanings

If the accompanying guidebook gives its own interpretations of the elements, write or discuss these, include your own opinion on whether you think these are accurate or fitting. For example, in traditional decks, water is the emotional state.

But, perhaps in a sports-themed deck water is nourishment since you need to stay hydrated when active. If the guide book does not give ideas as to what the elements mean then write your own ideas based on the theme of the deck for example, in a deck based on pirates water would be a means of travel and freedom rather than emotions.

Major Arcana as a Suit

When I work with Tarot I consider the Major Arcana the suit of Spirit because this correlates with my spiritual practices of the four basic elements: earth, air, water, fire and the fifth element of spirit.

Do you view the Major Arcana as its own suit or is it something entirely its own? If you do view it as a suit then what suit or element is it? (In some Asian cultures there are five elements such as: wood, water, metal, fire, earth).

Majors and Elements

The Major Arcana is not divided into a basic archai or elemental correspondence, but in the imagery and scenes an element might be more prominent then in another or all of theme might be in a single card.

For example, The Magician has all the tools of the elements on a table in front of him but in Temperance water is prominent with the angel pouring a liquid from one cup to another and she is standing in water.

The Star card also depicts water more prominently, although the person has one foot in the water and one on land. Look at each card and think about what element is prominent in it.

How do these elemental depictions add to the reading of the card, or what does the lack of any elements mean in reading the card?

Oracle Decks

If using a deck that is not based on the Rider-Waite system and does not have suit or elemental distinctions are there other ways that the cards can be divided?

For example, if using an animal deck are there birds (air), terrestrial (earth), or sea (water) animals?

If using a deck based on deities are there those who reign over water (Poseidon or Sedna) and those of the air (Mercury or Hermes)?

How about a deck using objects only—can they be divided into modes of travel, communication, or personal needs?

NUMERICAL CORRESPONDENCES

Numbers have a long history and are prominent in religion, folktales, superstitions, mythology, and theology and Tarot is no exception.

Each of the basic number 0-9 or 1-10 (depending on how you view the numerical scale) has meaning and the Pip cards (the numbered cards in the Minor Arcana) all use numerical correspondences in the reading of them.

Quite often a person can combine only the elemental meaning and the numerical meaning of a card to get a basic reading of it (without even looking at imagery).

Take the Four of Cups for example. The number four is one of stability and cups are of emotions so we have "an emotionally stable state of mind" (or something of the sort). The Two of Pentacles can mean balance in finances or between work and social life.

Looking for patterns of numbers can be a very crucial aspect in a reading, often they can tell more about the results than the cards themselves.

For example, if a person is trying to achieve success or happiness and in the reading the number two shows up a lot it could indicate that they need balance in their life in order to get the desired results. Once they balance things out it will work in their favor.

Noticing what numbers are missing is also a good indication as to what a person needs to do or what may be missing from their life.

For example, in the same type of question as above, if everything else shows up favorably indicating that a person is on the right path for their desired outcome, but the reader notices that while there is a pattern of 1, 3, 4, 5, 6 in the cards it should be noticed that what is missing is "balance" (two) and until this is achieved the person will not get their desired results.

Looking at odd and even cards is also important. Even cards denote femininity, a negative outcome, and stability. Odds denote a positive outcome, instability, and masculinity. In a reading, all or mostly all evens could indicate that the answer is not favorable and a reading with mostly odd or all odd numbered cards can indicate the answer is favorable.

Universal VS. Personal Correspondences

As with all things, there is a universal meaning for the numbers. Write the meanings down or just think about them, and then compare them to your own personal correspondences to the numbers. Do you agree with the universal meanings? Why or Why not?

Minors VS Majors

In readings, the numbers of Major Arcana are not often brought into consideration thought the cards are numbered. However, the Major Aracana numbered 1-10 often compare to their numerical counterpart in the Minor Arcana.

Pull the Major Arcana of these numbers and compare or contrast the meanings of a card in the Minor Arcana with the same number. For example, two is a number of "balance" and The High Priestess in the Major Arcana is numbered two—does she also represent balance in some way?

Key Words for the Numbers

Write a few keywords for the numbers 1-10. This is different then writing key words for the card as a whole; this is based just on the numbers instead.

For example, a four might have key words such as: stability, archetypal family, four elements, etc. But it would not have: happiness, joy, etc. The words must correlate to the number only.

Key Phrases for the Numbers

As with the idea above, try writing a key phrase or sentence for each of the cards. Key phrases can be clichés, a sentence, or just a phrase but based on the number only.

For example, the Fool might be "there is no beginning and no ending" which indicates the number 0 in that it is a complete circle with no beginning and no ending. But a key phrase would not be "feeling optimistic" as this does not indicate a number correlation.

Key Words for Even and Odd

Create your own list of keywords for even and odds. Take all of the pip cards and write the key words for all of the ones, the twos, etc (which you may already have if you did the previous exercise).

Then, group together all the keywords from the even numbered cards and all the keywords from the odd numbered cards and look for similarities.

Try to reduce this to five keywords that accurately depict all the even cards and a list that accurately depicts all the odd cards.

For example, if in your list of keywords for the numbers 1, 3, 5, 7, and 9 you have words like: action, movement, activity, commotion, motion then reduce those to one word of: Action.

Numerical Correspondence for Majors 11-21 & 0

We already know that the Fool and all the cards from eleven on up don't have a numerical correspondence in the Minor Arcana and often the numbers themselves do not have numerical meaning.

But, this doesn't mean we cannot contribute meaning to them based on personal feelings or individual spiritual beliefs.

For example, The Fool is number zero; often seen as a number of cycles in that there is no beginning and no end. Does this fit with the Fool card? What about the number 13, is it an unlucky or lucky number for you?

Based on personal experience or card imagery, what correspondences can you come up with for the other numbers?

Court Numerical Correspondences

Like the Major Arcana the courts might have a number on the card but the numerical correspondence is often neglected. However, Pages would be eleven, knights are twelve, Queens thirteen and King's fourteen.

Think about the cards and give meaning to these numbers and then compare their numerical equivalent in the Major Arcana. Do the pages show any resemble to the Justice card in the Major Arcana?

Combine Elements and Numbers

Now that you have an idea of the meanings associated with the elements and the numbers combine the two meanings. Choose a few cards and practice combining the meanings in order to read the card.

By knowing that water means emotions and aces are new beginnings a person can read a card without even looking at any other imagery (this makes it helpful in reading decks that don't depict scenes but just numbers and elemental symbols).

In the example given, if we see an Ace of Cups we automatically know "new beginnings" and "emotions" so the base interpretation might be "you will start feeling new emotions."

Oracle Decks

Often oracle cards are not numbered so we might not initially see any numerical correspondences. However, there may be certain numbers of things in the picture.

For example, if we know the number two means balance and

snakes are seen as good versus evil then if there are two snakes in a card this might mean we need to balance the good with the bad. If there are seven angels we might read this card as divine guidance or intervention will come into play Look at the symbols, animals, objects and people and at how many of them there are and write or discuss how this adds to the meaning.

PICTORIAL SYMBOLS

Symbols are everywhere and we use them daily, perhaps without realizing it. Recognizing symbols is something we do on a daily basis from looking for the stairs or elevator to road signs as we're driving.

While watching television or reading a book we might pick up on subtle cues of symbols that evoke emotions or particular responses. Our minds are probably taking in an array of symbols constantly and registering these in some fashion, and we may not even be aware of it.

In Tarot the symbols can enhance a reading by giving readers little cues as to what emotions, feelings, ideas, or meanings the card is trying to convey.

Aside from the elemental symbols of pentacles, swords, cups, and wands there are other cues in each and every card such as hearts, keys, food, gifts, tools, animals, styles of clothing, nudity, crowns, thrones, wreaths or other adornments and décor, and so much more.

There may be several dozen symbols in one deck and different people might respond to or see symbols that another doesn't.

A symbol is, basically, something that stands for or represents something else and can be abstract or direct. It can also be a written or printed sign or character that represents a specific context, such as in math with equation and mathematical symbols.

Our alphabet is essentially a series of twenty-six symbols that we've given meaning

We also understand grammatical symbols such as the ampersand (&) for and or the 'at' (@) symbol used in Tweets and email.

Symbols are even used in psychoanalysis with dream images or therapists and psychologists using symbols to determine a person's mental status (such as the Rorschach inkblot tests).

And, in Tarot, symbols can give us cues to the cards. It is not critical to look at *everything* as a symbol. For example, a chair might just be a chair but if something stands out as being symbolic then it probably is.

Look at the symbols in the card and either apply intuition, the universal meaning, or both methods to determine just what it is doing there and how it applies to the meaning. To get acquainted with Tarot or with a specific deck, sift through each card taking a close look and seeing what symbols are represented.

Seek and Find

What patterns and symbols do you see repeated within a deck? Write down a list of the symbols and then, in turn, you can work with each of those cards with the symbols.

For example a list might be: hearts, moons or stars; and write what cards these appear in. Don't forget intangible things such as: horse riding, flying, swimming.

Universal VS. Personal Correspondences

What is the universal or stereotypical meaning attached to the symbol(s)? Do these typically fit the meaning of the card or not? What are your own personal interpretations for the symbols depicted in Tarot?

Repeated Symbols

Pick one symbol and sort through the deck pulling all the cards with that symbol. Look at each card and write what that symbol means for that particular card.

For example, the sun in the Sun card is large and indicates optimism, outlook is good, etc. But if there is a card where the sun is small and perhaps half hidden behind something then it might mean that things will be looking up (sunny) eventually, just not right now.

Or, if a sun is rising or setting this might indicate different phases in a person's life. Try this with several different symbols at different times and discuss or write down your observations.

Connections

After doing the above activity, look at all the cards with that symbol in it. How does it connect all the cards? For example, if you are studying doors as a symbol, do all the cards with a door in the scene have similar correlations such as openings, closings, opportunities, or crossroads?

Enhances the Card's Meaning

Picking one particular symbol again, think about how that symbol enhances a card when compared to the elemental meaning, the numerical correspondence, or other key words?

For example, a door in the two of cups might indicate that by balancing (two) one's emotions (water) new opportunities will arise (door).

Alternate Symbols

Choose a few symbols at random (or using the ones you did for the previous activities) and determine what other symbols might have been used to represent the same meaning.

For example, a wagon or some other vehicular device would represent travel but a road in the scene could represent the same concept.

Symbol Reading

Lay out a simple one or three-card spread and interpret the reading using only the symbols in the card and not the elemental or numerical significance.

Write or discuss your observations on if you feel this is still an accurate reading, whether cards can be interpreted accurately, or what the significance is on the symbols read just on their own.

Personal Symbol Choices

If you were creating your own card, deck, or theme what

symbols would you like to use in a card? What symbols would you like to see that maybe are not depicted in the deck? What symbols would you have used to convey the same meaning in a card?

For example, if a shamrock denotes luck would you have used a horseshoe if creating the deck? Perhaps a horse shoe as a luck symbol is more accurate in a Knight card since they ride horses.

Oracle Decks

In Oracle decks there might not be full scenes depicted but might be just symbols representing a meaning or might be pictures of animals or deities only. But, even within Oracle decks there may be symbols that don't stand out immediately.

Look at the cards and try to find symbolism in the way an object, person or animal is positioned. Or look for less obvious symbols such as a tree or lake in the background of a picture of a beaver. What do these mean for that card?

Zodiac Symbols

As you look at the cards look for symbols, animals, people, or objects that might depict the zodiac signs and write or discuss how this adds to the interpretation of the card.

For example, in the Page of Cups there is a man holding a chalice with a fish poking his head out. If we interpret this as a sign of Pisces what does this add to the card's meaning?

COLOR CORRESPONDENCES

Colors can play an important role in interpreting the cards and, in fact, can be just as important as numerology or symbols.

Numerous studies have been done to show the effect of colors on our emotions or psyche and while different colors affect people differently there are universal messages behind the basic colors such as seeing red as either a warning or the color of love. Green usually denotes money and blue is often a peaceful color.

The colors are even divided into "temperatures" such as cold colors being blues, greens, and purples and warm colors being reds, oranges and yellows.

Colors can give us indications of what feeling or emotion a specific card is conveying or even tell us more specifically what feeling or message is behind a symbol.

For example, the Fool card is bright colors indicating enthusiasm or exuberance and the dog, who is barking a warning, is colored red which is a universal color meaning either danger, beware, or stop.

Colors are used often in Paganism or New Age practices with color correspondences being used for specific spell intents or purposes.

If looking for a new job a green candle might be burned, or if wanting to find a dream home a brown (earthy) candle might be used. Knowing basic color correspondences adds yet one more tool for reading and understanding the cards in Tarot. The back of this book has a list of basic colors and their correspondences.

Universal VS. Personal Correspondences

Discuss or write down the universal meaning of the colors. Then, write or discuss your own personal meanings of the colors. How do they compare or contrast?

For example, orange is vibrant and energetic but does orange, to you, instead mean chaotic, loud and disruptive? How do these meanings play into a reading or interpretation of a card?

Colors in the Cards

Tarot decks are often very colorful, although there are those that are made in black and white or only a few colors (I have one colored with reds, whites and blacks only) and not every color is going to mean something, for example the color of ordinary clothing might not have any meaning.

But, the color of a wedding dress of funeral garb might. The suits might also have specific hues such as water cards being made up of blues, greens or purples.

Look through the deck and pick out objects, clothing, scenery, etc that you feel the color is projecting an idea or saying something about the card. You can also look at the overall color scheme, is it bright and cheery or all dark and muted colors? Pick out five-ten cards (or the whole deck if feeling ambitious) and describe the color patterns and what they might mean.

Colors Telling a Story

With those same cards write or discuss whether the colors enhance or detract from the meaning of the card. For example, if the card is about being lively, new, and energetic but the colors are browns and blacks does the color scheme fit the meaning of the card?

Compare Symbols & Colors

Look at a variety of symbols in the decks and check to see if they are colored the same. For example, a heart is typically colored red, but is there a card where the heart is a different color, perhaps black? How does this change the meanings of the symbols?

Your Color Choices

If using a "color your own deck", describe what colors or color schemes you would use (pastels, traditional colors, neutrals, using different shades of one color, etc.) and what this color scheme would mean to the deck.

Also, consider the idea that if you change colors of symbols does it change the meaning of the symbol? For example, butterflies mean change and metamorphosis but they mean this no matter the color or the patterns. But, if you color a sun black or brown how does this affect its meaning? Why or why not?

Black and White Decks

Some decks are known as "black and white" decks and have no colors other than shades of white, gray or black. How do you think this lack of color adds or takes away from the deck?

If you don't have a black and white deck look for pictures online or just use your own personal feelings about how you think this would make you feel (to use a deck without color). You can also try this with a Poker deck which is only black and red suits.

Color Key Words

Think of the basic colors of the rainbow (replacing indigo and violet with purple) and basic neutrals such as black, brown, white and grey. Write key words that you feel represent the colors best. These can be based on universal or personal correspondences.

Color Key Phrases

Taking the key words above, write a key phrase that encompasses the ideas or concepts conveyed by the key words. For example, if your key words for orange are curiosity, fiery, and energetic the key phrase might be "an energetic and fiery sense of curiosity which may lead to answers, or to trouble."

THE PEOPLE OF TAROT

Some Tarot or Oracle decks may have only animals or only objects or symbols. But if there are people in the pictures you can bet they have significance. When learning Tarot or becoming familiar with a new dec

k it is always useful to pay attention to what the people are doing. Granted, we know that the royal family has importance and we know in the Majors that the people have importance.

However, what about in the Six of Cups or the Ten of Swords; what do the people in those cards represent? What about the Three of Swords in which the female is often depicted blindfolded and with arms crossed?

Each person, how they look or dress, what they are doing, and their interactions with the scenery and other people all can have a significant role in reading the cards.

In every walk of life and in every culture we pay attention to the little nuances of people: the way they stand, sit, or talk; their posture and their gestures or facial expressions; the way they dress or act.

We see a lot about people just by interacting and certain gestures, stances or postures can mean different things in different cultures. A pose we may see as relaxed might be one of disdain in a different culture or sitting with a toe pointing towards someone can be considered an insult. It is nearly impossible to describe and define all of the little things that people do and what they mean to us, so readers are on their own for determining just what a person or card is conveying based on what the people are doing.

But, generally we think of a person sitting as relaxed, whereas someone who stands perfectly straight is trying to give a good impression. A slouched person might have poor self-esteem, and someone with their head down or hands on their head might be feeling dejected. Someone with their chin on their hand might be a thinker, and one looking up towards the sky might be over-optimistic or naïve.

In addition to how they sit or stand, there are things to consider such as how they look. We are told to "not judge a book by its cover" but that is what we do, both literally and figuratively. If a person is dressed nice we assume they have money, dressed poorly and we assume they are poor.

Someone unclean and unkempt might not be one we approach to ask for help, the time, or to make the acquaintance of. We also judge people by their interactions with others. Do they stand too close to people or keep their distance? Are they rude or polite? Do they have a soft or loud voice?

All of these give us an idea (whether right or wrong) about a person and cause us to form our own opinions about them. Granted, in a picture we don't know how they talk or walk but there are plenty of other cues they can give us.

Noting if they are masculine or feminine is also important. Stereotypically men are seen as strength, fatherly, the protectors, stern, and are dominant.

Odd numbers are considered masculine and masculinity is considered the yang of yin and yang. Male dominated readings could indicate that a man will help influence the income or that a person may need to take on the personalities of the stereotypical male in order to get the desired outcome.

Women are stereotypically maternal, motherly, soft, sympathetic, easy-going, gentle, and sensitive. Even numbers are feminine and femininity is the yin of yin and yang. A female dominated reading could mean that a woman is going to help with the desired outcome or that the person needs to embrace their feminine side in order to get the desired outcome.

Paying attention to how the men and women interact in one card is also important in that it may tell more about the querant or their situation. If a card has several people in it look and see how they are interacting.

An example is the Four of Wands and a couple holding hands may show them as equal partners in their endeavors. But a card where one sits and one stands may indicate that one person is more dominant than the other.

By taking a look at what the people in Tarot are doing, how they do it, and who they are doing it with can tell a lot about a card and can, in fact, give a more in-depth reading than the symbols, numbers, or other correspondences. Take some time to look at the cards with people in them and see just what it is they are doing, I guarantee that each person has their own story or message to tell.

Find the People

Pull out cards with people in them and write/discuss a brief description of how the people look or what they might be doing. Keep in mind to think about which way they are facing, their posture, their clothing, their actions, facial expressions, etc.

People Interpretations

With the same cards as above write/discuss an interpretation for each card based on just the actions, style, or appearance of the people. You can also read the interpretations in the guide book that comes with a deck and write/discuss whether you agree or disagree with the interpretations.

People of the Suit

Look at the people in each suit: are the activities or mannerisms of the people in the cards accurate for the meaning of the suit? For example, are the ones in an earth suit all toiling in the garden, working, or involved with money? If they are not doing the actions the element depicts do you think there is a reason for this.

For example, if in a swords card—which often means communication—are the people obviously not communicating but look as if they are too busy working to talk? This could mean that the persons in the querant's life need to find time to communicate with each other.

Actions and Movements

For each card (or choose just a few) write/discuss about the person's actions, their mannerisms, gestures, facial expressions, etc. Are they looking 'away from the camera' or towards it, what is the significance of where or how they are gazing (looking down usually means despondent, looking over shoulder may be cautious or frightened). Take in every little action or movement, even if it is just one finger pointed up or a toe pointing out.

Relationships

Look at the cards you have pulled out. Is the person alone or is it a couple? Is it a group of people all seemingly to interact (like the 5 of Wands or 3 of Cups) or is it a crowd in the background and one person standing out (such as Death). Do the people appear to be a family? Are they of the same age or different ages? Look at all these aspects and write or discuss how this affects the meaning of the card or what it says for an interpretation.

Character Appearances

How are the people dressed? Is their appearance shabby or dressed well? What is their hair and clothing like? Are they dressed better or worse than others in the picture? Does their dress fit the scene, for example is it a lavish castle but the people dressed poorly?

In some decks or cards the people are nude, what does this say about them or the meaning of the card or are they wearing too much clothing (indicating they are hiding something, whereas nude is vulnerable or nothing to hide).

Conversations

Look at each of the people in the cards and discuss what conversation they may be having with each other. If there is only one person in a card you can do one of three things (or all three):

1) what is the person thinking?

2) what would the person say to you?

3) pick another card with people, what conversation would occur between the two cards?

Artist Depiction

Did the artist use the people in the card to depict the universal meaning appropriately, For example, the Fool card is of new beginnings, youthfulness and adventure...but if the artist depicts the Fool old, fat and lazy then this does not fit with its meaning.

In what other ways could an artist have depicted the people and still fit with the general meaning of the card?

Male vs. Female

Men and women are both depicted in cards, and sometimes they can indicate an actual male or female or other times they might imply the stereotypical traits of that gender such as getting in touch with a masculine or feminine side.

For example, in a male querant's reading a lot of women might come up and depending on the question it could either mean too many women are influencing his life (mom, sisters, girlfriend) or it may mean that he needs to be more sensitive and soft in order to get the resolution or desired outcome.

Pick a few cards and write or discuss the masculine and feminine personality traits of each card or how the men and women interact with each other.

Write the stereotypical qualities of men and women and compare these with the actions of the people in the card. For example, men are considered the stronger of the two but is there a women depicted doing work requiring strength?

People Today

How do the personas depict real-life personas of people today? For example, would the Hanged Man be anyone who doesn't fit the "norms" of society such a transgender, a Goth, or other extreme lifestyle, or would he be an acrobat or circus performer (because of his unusual position in the tree). How about the Fool—perhaps an actor or entertainer?

Similar Actions

Pull out all the cards in which a person is doing a similar act (riding a horse, dancing, etc) and write/discuss how these cards are related or linked together and what that act means in each card.

Inter-Mingling

Pull out several cards with people on them and describe how a person(s) in the card would interact with the people in the other cards.

For example, how would the High Priestess, the Magician and the children in the 6 of Cups all interact together? Do this for several sets of cards. This can also lead to story prompts or creative writing which can be used in a later section of this book.

Categories

Sort cards with people into groups such as those depicting family units, royalty, respected positions, children, laborers, couples, etc. Some cards may fit for more than one category so just choose which one they fit into the best.

Write or discuss why you feel those people fit into that placed category (for example family units are shown by people of different ages or royalty are depicted as such by their clothes or in a castle setting.

The People in Your Neighborhood

Look around at officials, positions of office, co-workers, and neighbors and based on their personality, your connection to them, or their position in the city (mayor, fireman, policeman) sort through a deck and look for cards that fit with that person.

You don't necessarily have to know the person in order to choose a card. For example, a Mayor might be like one of the kings in the court cards, or a fireman is the Tower since it is often depicted burning and fireman deal with tragic events almost daily.

Advise Me

Choose several cards with people in them and think about the meaning of the card and the actions or appearance of the people. Think about what the person in the card would advise you of.

For example, if you are wondering about changing careers and are looking at the Fool what advice might he give you? How does this compare and contrast to the advise that the man in the Four of Pentacles might give?.

In The Court's Shoes

The court cards are often all seen in similar positions such as the Knights on horses, Pages on walking somewhere, and the Kings and Queens are on thrones. Look at each of the court cards and imagine what it would be like to "be in their shoes." Which role do you fulfill or would like to fulfill and why?

ANIMALS IN TAROT

Typically when we think of animal symbolism it is the stereotypical associations we have as a society such as foxes are crafty, dogs are loyal, cats are independent, etc.

Dream dictionaries are filled with animals and their and there are plenty of books in New Age sections that discuss animal symbolism. Ted Andrews' book "Animal Speak" (Llewellyn Publications) is perhaps the most well-known and the most comprehensive book on animal symbolism and totems.

Books on superstitions and folklore will also have a plethora of entries related to animals and the folklore, superstition, or the symbolism attached to them.

When reading cards it is important to look at the animals not just for their symbolism but also for their color, their actions and movements, and their interactions with either other animals or people.

As stated before, the dog in the Fool card is barking a warning to the Fool who is about to go over a cliff. In The Knight cards all the horses are in various states of movement (full gallop, slow pace, etc).

In cards that depict only animals we can look at secondary animals such as bird flying overhead where the main image is of a dog.

Like all else, there are universal correspondences to animals but their meaning also changes depending on a person's individual, religious, or cultural experiences.

I have not included an appendix of animals at the end of this book s there are simply too many to try and delve into. I recommend the above book or other books on animal symbolism, or base it on common knowledge and personal or spiritual experiences when performing the following exercises.

Find the animals

Sort through the deck and pull out all the cards that have animals on them, make sure to look for animal imagery such a statue or maybe there is a carving or a painting that has an animal.

Make a list of the animals seen in the cards. Is there one animal that is used more often then the others or is there a particular theme to the animals used (all domestic animals, or all exotic, for example)?

This activity will work for all decks including oracle decks (except for decks that are all-animal cards).

Universal VS. Personal

Looking at all the cards with animals that you have pulled, write or discuss the universal symbolism of the animals and compare them to your personal correspondences to them.

Animal Key Words

Write key words for the animals in each of the cards you pulled. Key words for one animal may change depending on what it is doing in the card.

For example, a dog laying at the feet of its master shows loyalty and companionship but a dog in another card snarling and snapping is showing a sign of aggression or severe warning.

Compare and contrast the key words for one set of animals (key words for all the dogs, then all the cats, etc) and see how they compare or contrast.

Animal Key Phrases

Based on your key words above write key phrases for the animals as a whole; for example, "dogs in Tarot mean loyalty and companionship."

If their key words vary greatly from card to card then write a positive and negative key phrase for the animals.

In the example given in the previous entry we might have the statement about dogs being loyalty but a negative counterpart might be "dogs are a sign of a sever warning that something bad is sure to come."

Animals and Elements

Look at the suits in a deck and what animals are depicted in those suits. For example, are the animals in water or cups suit all sea, ocean or lake animals? Is the earth element portrayed with forest or terrestrial animals? Are air element would be birds and fire might be lizards, dragons, or just any desert animal.

Does the deck portray this or not. If not, how could the deck have portrayed this but still fit in the theme of the deck?

Categories

Sort all the cards into groups according to animals they share (there may be some cross-sharing if more than one animal appears in a card).

Categories might include: mammals, reptiles, birds. Other ways to categorize might be pets, domestic (cows, horses), or wild animals; indigenous or exotic, large versus small animals, or whatever other categories you can come up with.

Write or discuss the significance of the categories and how the animals all compare or contrast in that category.

Compare and Contrast

You may see one animal depicted in several cards, set these cards aside and thinking on the interpretation or meaning of the card (either the universal or your own personal) write or discuss the similarities and differences between the same animal in different cards?

For example the Moon and the Fool cards both have a dog but their meaning in each card is different.

Animal Interactions

Often the animals are not alone but they are with people or other animals.

Pull all the cards where animals are in a scene with someone else or another animal and write or discuss how they interact with people or other animals in the card.

If there is a card where an animal is alone then write or discuss why it is alone and perhaps how it feels or how it would interact with animals in another card.

Animal Actions & Movements

What are the mannerisms, actions, and appearances of each animal? How are their actions affecting the scene or other living things around them? Do their actions aid in interpreting the card?

Choosing a Different Animal

Some animals might have similar symbolism such as dogs are loyal but a horse, among other things, might also be seen as loyal.

Choose a few cards, randomly if you want, and determine what other animal could have been in that card that would represent the same concept, idea, or emotion.

Artist Depiction

How do you feel about the artist depiction of the animal? Is the animal small and insignificant or does it have a major role in the card? Did the artist depict the animal accurately for its universal symbolism, for example dogs represent loyalty but is a dog running away from someone? Or, swans mean beauty so if a card has a swan does it meaning of inner beauty or outward appearances?

Meaning of Card Enhanced

Write or discuss whether you feel the meaning of the card is enhanced or hindered by the depiction of the animal and how that meaning could have been represented without the use of the animal.

For example, in Strength she holds a lion's mouth shut with her bare hands, which means that strength is not always shown as physical strength. How could this have been represented without the lion's image?

Choose a Different Animal

Select three to five cards either at random or by choice and write or discuss how a different animal could have been used to still represent the same symbolism.

For example, if a swan reflects beauty in a card could the artist have chosen a different animal, such as peacock, to represent beauty as well? Or, select three to five cards and mentally swap the animals.

If you choose the Sun, Strength, and Fool which have a horse, lion, and dog (in that order) mentally swap those animals around. How does the Fool change if it is horse or lion next to him? What does a dog or horse mean in Strength instead of a lion?

Advise Me

Choose three to five cards from the deck with different animals on them. If the animals could speak what advice would they be giving you or what kind of conversation would you have?

Animal Oracle

For all-animal oracles pull out any card that shows another animal in the scene and write why you think this animal is there. For example, in a picture of a bird is there also a worm?

This might indicate a sense of nourishment in addition to what the bird represents.

Also look at the types of animals, are there animals from several different terrains (desert, forest, tundra, ocean, etc) or are the animals all exotic or all domestic? Write or discuss the meaning behind why a secondary animal may appear or why the animals in a deck are all of a similar category, or why they are not if they are animals from several different areas.

Minor Arcana: Pips

The Minor Arcana is the mundane world; this is the world we exist in on a daily basis and the cards represent a series of everyday feelings, events and situations. Meaning "little secrets," the Minor Arcana is made up of fourteen cards; numbered 1-10 and then four court cards.

The numbered cards are known as 'pips' or suits and are similar to the cards seen in a regular playing deck (sometimes referred to as a poker deck). Each suit also represents an element, social class, an emotional state, or personality traits.

There are hundreds of varieties of Tarot and there are several versions of poker or standard decks as well. Some countries still see decks with Tarot-like images used in certain card games and other card game decks have different suits.

In Italian decks the suits might be cups, coins, clubs and swords; German suits are seen as hearts or roses, bells, acorns and leaves; French inspired decks (such as are sold in the US) are hearts, diamonds, clubs and spades.

The suits we see in Rider-Waite Tarot with pentacles, swords, wands and cups were derived from the Golden Dawn system of esotericism and occultism but the depiction of each element is left up to the authors of the decks and may coincide with the overall theme of the deck.

Minor Arcana cards in a reading typically mean the answer to the question or the solution will occur in a shorter amount of time and that it is materialistically or physically based; in other words, something tangible.

If a lot of minor cards show up in a reading it can mean that the situation involves a simple solution or that the events will unfold quickly or that the querant has control, to an extent, over the situation and can achieve the desired results based on the decisions they make. It could also mean that the question and outcome is based on materialistic needs.

Of course, this is may not always be the rule depending on the card's position in the layout, the reader's interpretation or the situation being evaluated.

If there are more pips in the layout than courts then it may mean that the solution relies solely on the querant's shoulders (the reverse, that is if there are more courts, can mean that others will step in and help the querant).

However, as will be discussed later, the lack of any courts could mean that a person needs to seek advice, or the lack of any pips may mean that a person needs to take more of a position in their own situation and ask others to back off.

Minor Arcana Importance

Based on what you know about the Minor Arcana from either this book, the guide book accompanying a deck, or prior knowledge write or discuss what you feel is the importance of the Minor Arcana Pip cards.

Universal VS Personal Correspondences

What are the universal correspondences for the pips as a suit and what are your personal correspondences, do they correlate with each other or do you have other ideas about what the cards mean?

Ace-Ten Descriptions

Write/discuss a description for each of the cards based on scenery or imagery only, as if you were describing a picture in a book.

Do not write an interpretation of what the card means, just a description of what you are seeing.

For example, the Ace of Chalices card might be described as "a single cup sits on a cloud with a halo of light around it."

Weather & Seasons

Look at each of the cards and pull out all the ones that show a definite sense of weather or seasons. Write what weather or season is being shown and how this affects the interpretation of the card.

For example, sunny is often depicted as optimistic and stormy might be bad times are evident.

If all the cards in a deck have indications of weather or seasons then choose only a few cards at random and do this exercise.

Ace-Ten Key Words

If feeling very ambitious, write a few keywords for every card in the deck but, just as practice you can try writing key words for just a small sample, especially if doing this as a lesson or group activity.

Sit with your deck and pull out all of the same number in the suits, such as all the Aces, and write key words for them perhaps spending one day on the Aces, one day on the Twos, and so on.

Ace-Ten Key Phrases

As with the idea above, try writing a key phrase or sentence for each of the cards, or if doing this as a lesson or group activity pick a few cards from each suit.

Key phrases can be clichés, a sentence describing the scene, feelings invoked by the scene, etc.

This is a lesson in interpretation and there is no right or wrong, just choose phrases that help you interpret the card.

Ace-Ten Interpretations

Using the key words, phrases, and descriptions you have written with the other exercises write your own interpretation for each of the cards in the deck.

Keep these interpretations in a book where you can access them easily and quickly as they may help you in doing readings or can be used as a quick study guide for brushing up on the meanings of the cards.

Random Interpretation

If time or energy does not merit writing an interpretation for all the cards, pick 1-3 at random and write interpretations for them. This can be done several times until all the cards have been done.

If you do this exercise several times and get a card you wrote on previously write a new interpretation for it, and then compare that to the previous one or choose a new card.

Masculine Vs. Feminine Traits

Look at the cards that have men and women in them and compare or contrast the qualities or traits that are being exhibited by them.

For example, are all the women seen in stereotypical female roles?

Or, think of the reverse and decide what feminine qualities a male in a card may be exhibiting and so on. If the cards are all one gender describe how it still entails both the feminine and masculine qualities.

Minor Arcana Feelings & Emotions

Generally speaking, the Pip cards convey everyday feelings, emotions, and mundane tasks or activities.

Select three to five cards from each suit either by choice or at random, and write down your own personal ides on what feelings, emotions or activities are being represented.

Mundane and Magical

Can the pips also depict the magical or spiritual sides to life? Do they correspond to the courts? For example, the man in the Two of Wands looks sort of like an Emperor (Major Arcana) or a King (Courts).

Does his card have similarities to those cards in their meanings? Is there a Minor Arcana with a similar meaning to The Hanged Man or Justice?

These correlations do not have to be a direct connection between the numbers of the Minor and the Major but can be based on appearance or traits of the card and/or the people in it.

Negative and Positive Traits

Pick five-to-ten cards at random and write/discuss key words or phrases for that card using negative traits or words (grief, despair, regret, etc).

Now, go back and look at those same cards and write or discuss positive traits or words (happiness, success, joy). How do these negative and positive traits work for reading the card?

This can be a real challenge and gets us away from thinking all cards are either-or when really they are ambiguous—can be either positive or negative depending on several circumstances.

This also helps when deciding to use reversals later on, although it does not have to be done using reversals.

Minor Arcana: Court Cards

The court cards are part of the Minor Arcana and are four cards depicting a certain hierarchy, in some decks this hierarchy is seen as a royal court. In RWS decks it is Page, Knight, Queen and King. Some decks replace the Page and the Knight with Prince and Princess.

Court cards are the people in our lives that have influence on us such as friends, relationships, family, co-workers, etc. They represent actual persons or personality-types and could indicate that either someone with those personalities will enter into the querant's life or that the querant needs to adapt the personalities of that court card to get the desired result.

The courts also represent certain age levels such as Pages being people ages 1-25; Knights 25-50; Queens 25+; and Kings 25+. Pages and Queens represent women and Knights or Kings represent men.

Of course, like everything else in Tarot this is subjective as a Page may not mean a woman but just embracing maternal or feminine characteristics, perhaps a stern male that needs to be more sympathetic.

When focusing on the Court Cards think about their royal positions: Pages are seen as messengers; Knights are fighting battles or on a quest; King's and Queen's are rulers—consider what all of them might be ruling, the message conveyed, or the quest they are on.

Also, consider elemental cues with the Courts. Often the court cards are the hardest to read, so looking at the elements can help.

For example, you know fire/swords means communication or action so how does that help in interpreting the Queen of Swords? Also consider the ages of the courts and how this can help interpret its meaning.

The best thing I have seen for helping in interpreting these cards is to combine their purpose or role in the court and their elemental realm:

Pages are messengers so the Page of Pentacle brings messages of a physical nature (about your health, career, etc); Page of Wands brings messages of a spiritual nature; Page of Cups brings messages of an emotional nature; and Page of Swords brings messages of an intellectual nature.

Knights are on quests or represent adventure so a Knight of Pentacle brings physical adventure or rescue; Knight of Wands brings spiritual adventure or rescue; Knight of Cups brings emotional adventure or rescue; Knight of Swords brings intellectual adventure or rescue.

Queens are considering motherly and nurturing and the Queen

of Pentacles nurtures and protects the physical; Queen of Wands nurtures and protects the spiritual; Queen of Cups the emotional and Swords the intellectual.

King's are rulers and leaders. The King of Pentacles shows physical defense or leadership; King of Wands spiritual defense or leadership; King of Cups emotional defense or leadership and King of Swords intellectual defense or leadership.

Court cards in a reading usually show the personality of a person who may be involved, or will be involved, in the querant's situation.

Too many courts in a reading can indicate that too many people are involved in the querant's situation and s/he may need to tell them to back off so s/he can figure things out.

Or, it could mean that the other people in the querant's life are trying to direct the outcome in their favor (such as a pushy mom wanting grandkids) or advice given by others that is unwarranted or unwanted. If the last card in the spread is a court card in may mean that someone else will make the final decision for you.

Court Card Importance

Write or discuss the significance or importance of the court cards in a chosen deck. How do they compare or contrast to court systems in other decks and are they appropriate for the theme of the deck? Why are they important?

Universal VS. Personal Correspondence

What are the universal correspondences for the courts and what are your personal correspondences, do they correlate with each other or do you have other ideas about what the cards mean?

Page—King Descriptions

Write/discuss a description for each of the cards based on scenery or imagery only, as if you were describing a picture in a book.

Do not write an interpretation of what the card means, just a description of what you are seeing. For example, a Page might be "a young man stands on a hilltop smiling."

Weather & Seasons

Look at each of the courts and pull out all the ones that show a definite sense of weather or seasons. Write what weather or season is being shown and how this affects the interpretation of the card.

Page—King Key Words

If feeling very ambitious, write a few keywords for every card in the deck but, just as practice you can try writing key words for just a small sample, especially if doing this as a lesson or group activity.

However, as a long-term project I suggest writing your own key words for each card. Sit with your deck and pull out all of the same position in the courts, such as all the Pages, and write key words for them.

Page—King Key Phrases

As with the idea above, try writing a key phrase or sentence for each of the cards, or if doing this as a lesson or group activity pick a few cards from each suit. Key phrases can be clichés, a sentence describing the scene, feelings invoked by the scene, etc.

This is a lesson in interpretation and there is no right or wrong, just choose phrases that help you interpret the card.

Page—King Interpretation

Using the Key Words, Phrases, and Descriptions you have written with the other exercises write your own interpretation for each of the cards in the deck.

Keep these interpretations in a book where you can access them easily and quickly as they may help you in doing readings or can be used as a quick study guide for brushing up on the meanings of the cards.

Random Interpretation

If time or energy does not merit writing an interpretation for all the cards, pick 1-3 at random and write interpretations for them. This can be done several times until all the cards have been done.

If you do this exercise several times and get a card you wrote on previously either choose a new one, or write a new interpretation for it and compare that to the previous one.

Masculine and Feminine Traits

Look at the stereotypical roles of the men and women in the courts and describe their feminine or masculine traits. Stereotypically a King can mean a male is in involved in the querant's situation, but this is not always so, sometimes a card can mean that a person will need or have the masculine traits of that card.

For example, if a female is asking about a getting a promotion she may turn up a King card which is telling her to be bold, slightly aggressive and have a "take charge" attitude in order to get the promotion.

How else can feminine and masculine traits be interpreted in a reading?

Court's Activities

Each of the positions of court's are typically depicted doing a similar activity.

For example, all the Kings and Queens are on thrones; the Pages are on foot; and the Knights are on horseback.

Look at each set of cards and write/discuss what these actions mean. How do the actions or poses of the court cards help you with the interpretation of the card?

Pay special attention to the Pages and the Knights as typically they are seen in different poses or actions whereas King's and Queen's are typically just sitting on thrones.

Courts in Medieval Times VS Modern Times

Many decks have their imagery based in Medieval times, knowing what you know about those times write your own view on the purpose of a Page, Knight, Queen and King.

If your deck depicts modern social positions or careers compare those to what you know of medieval court positions. You can also take each of the court positions and apply it to social positions or leadership of today. For example, knights could become soldiers and Kings as presidents. Or, take those positions and apply them to a business hierarchy, town or group council, or family hierarchy.

Negative and Positive Traits

Pick five-to-ten cards at random and write/discuss key words or phrases for that card using negative traits or words (grief, despair, regret, etc). Now, go back and look at those same cards and write or discuss positive traits or words (happiness, success, joy).

How do these negative and positive traits work for reading the card? This can be a real challenge and gets us away from thinking all cards are either-or when really they are ambiguous—can be either positive or negative depending on several circumstances.

This also helps if deciding to use reversals later on, although it does not have to be done using reversals.

MAJOR ARCANA

The Major Arcana is a suit unto itself made up of twenty-two cards numbered 0-21. They are sometimes referred to as 'trump' or 'triumph' cards and when Tarot and poker decks diverged into two separate things, the Major Arcana were left out of poker decks. The term literally means "big secrets"

It is often said that the Major Arcana is "The Fool's Journey" and that as he starts off on his journey he learns a lesson or gains knowledge and experience from each of the cards. In most decks the Major Arcana starts with the Fool card (numbers zero) and ends with the World (number twenty-one).

In some decks or cultures the reverse might be used with the suit 'starting' with the World and ending with the Fool.

The Major Arcana is cyclic and even though we start at one point and end with another we know that the cycle repeats. Think of the season: summer comes, then fades to autumn which fades to winter and then to spring. This leads us back to summer and the seasons repeat, every year it's the same pattern.

On a philosophical level when "one door closes, another opens" and we are always moving onto something new and different. Even death is part of this cycle, when we die it is the end of one thing and the beginning of something else.

The Major Arcana is not representative of an element like the suits in the Minor Arcana but rather it is of the spiritual realm.

This is the magical world, the world of the divine or of our inner consciousness. It is where we are on a spiritual, philosophical or intellectual level or where we will end up when the journey is done. They often represent the intuitive world, the realm of change, and are a reflection of the natural laws of physics, science and nature.

The figures on the cards are all archetypal—that is, cosmic stereotypes that serve as a framework for our basic understanding of the world.

Archetypes transcend the limits of time and place and yet they are in each of us, we only have to unlock them. The Major Arcana is like that, each of the aspects of the twenty-two cards is in each of us if we only embrace or tap into it.

We all have the tools we need to deal with life as in the Magician card or the quiet reserve and strength such as in the Strength card. Free will and reasonable thinking gives us choices as in the Lovers card and we all have the ability to win the race in the Chariot.

Major Arcana in a reading are very powerful and represent profound archetypal qualities that permeate humanity both individually and collectively.

When a Major Arcana turns up in a reading it often means a lesson needs to be learned in order to move onto the next level or phase. If a lot of Major Arcana cards show up it could indicate that the issue at hand is important and needs urgent attention or it may be a situation that can only be resolved with spiritual guidance or divine intervention.

In studying Tarot I recommend to people all the time to study one or two Major Arcana everyday. In my studies I did one per day, everyday. I read up on the meaning of the card in three different sources, then I studied the picture of the card, and then I wrote my own interpretation for it as well as little mnemonic tricks for remembering it.

For example, the Chariot card is about having the commitment, the intelligence, and the knowledge to win a race. It is not about who is fastest or who has brute force but knowing that if prepared and if calm and rational, anything is achievable.

To me this sounds like the Aesop Fable "The Tortoise and the Hare" in which the tortoise, though much slower, knows he can win because the hare is over-confident. Sure enough, the hare takes several naps while the tortoise continues on. The moral of the fable is "slow and steady wins the race." So, in my personal guidebook my mnemonic tip is "think of the tortoise and the hare: slow and steady wins the race."

The majors are, to me, very important in a Tarot deck (aside from oracle decks which may not have any distinction as majors and minors) and are worth the time to sit and study one card at a time.

Major Arcana Purpose

The Major Arcana is considered a spiritual journey and as we travel from the Fool to the World we gather the necessary tools and knowledge until we complete a cycle, only to start a new journey or cycle. Why then is the Major Arcana important to have? How does it help us spiritually and emotionally and how would a Tarot Deck be lacking if it did not have a Major Arcana?

Universal VS. Personal Correspondence

What are the universal correspondences for the Majors and what are your personal correspondences, do they correlate with each other or do you have other ideas about what the cards mean? You can try this with just a few random or chosen cards, but eventually you may want to try this with all the cards.

Major Arcana Description

Write/discuss a description for the card based on scenery or imagery only, as if you were describing a picture in a book.

Do not write an interpretation of what the card means, just a description of what you are seeing such as in the Magician card it might be described as such: "a man stands at a table or altar with various elemental tools in front of him".

Weather & Seasons

Look at each of the Major Arcana cards and pull out all the ones that show a definite sense of weather or seasons. Write what weather or season is being shown and how this affects the interpretation of the card.

Major Arcana Key Words

If feeling very ambitious, write a few keywords for every card in the deck but, just as practice you can try writing key words for just a small sample, especially if doing this as a lesson or group activity. Pick two to three cards from each suit, including the Major Arcana.

As a long-term project I suggest writing your own key words for each card. Sit with your deck and pull out all of the same number in the suits, such as all the Aces, and write key words for them. Continue until all the suits are done and then write for the Major Arcana by selecting a few cards each day.

Major Arcana Key Phrases

As with the idea above, try writing a key phrase or sentence for each of the cards, or if doing this as a lesson or group activity pick a few cards from each suit.

Key phrases can be clichés, a sentence describing the scene, feelings invoked by the scene, etc.

This is a lesson in interpretation and there is no right or wrong, just choose phrases that help you interpret the card.

For example, the Fool card can be the cliché "a fool and his money are soon parted" or "only fools fall in love;" or it could be based on the scene "a fool stands at the edge of a precipice ignoring a warning;" or a feeling that the card invokes such as "the fool is vibrant and optimistic but he is oblivious to what could do wrong."

Major Arcana Interpretation

Using the key words, phrases, and descriptions you have written with the other exercises write your own interpretation for each of the cards in the deck.

Keep these interpretations in a book where you can access them easily and quickly as they may help you in doing readings or can be used as a quick study guide for brushing up on the meanings of the cards.

Random Interpretation

If time or energy does not merit writing an interpretation for all the cards, pick 1-3 at random and write interpretations for them. This can be done several times until all the cards have been done.

If you do this exercise several times and get a card you wrote on previously write a new interpretation for it, and then compare that to the previous one or choose a new card.

Masculine and Feminine Traits

Some of the Major Arcana cards depict people, these are archetypes and who they depict is just as important as what they depict.

For all of the cards with people in them list masculine and feminine traits that can be associated with it. With the cards with no people such as the Moon or the Sun are there still masculine or feminine traits that can be seen? In the example given, often the Sun is associated with masculine energies or traits and the Moon is associated with feminine. Do the other cards have these traits as well and how?

From the Beginning to the End

Think about the journey we take as we travel through the Major Arcana. What do we know, experience or feel at the beginning of the journey? At the end of the journey of the Major Arcana what should we have learned or gained?

In Kabbalah practices the Major Arcana is sometimes said to go in reverse, we start with the World and journey back to the Fool.

How does this change the meanings of the card or the experience?

Major Arcana & Real Life

Go through the Major Arcana and adapt a popular icon, celebrity, TV show, movie, popular theme, event, or current news for each of the Majors.

For example, the Tower card might be the collapse of the Twin Towers or the Empress might be Angelina Jolie and her adopted and biological children. Perhaps the Judgment card is a reality show such as American Idol or America's Got Talent in which people are judged and voted off.

Negative and Positive Traits

Pick five-to-ten cards at random and write/discuss key words or phrases for that card using negative traits or words (grief, despair, regret, etc).

Now, go back and look at those same cards and write or discuss positive traits or words (happiness, success, joy). How do these negative and positive traits work for reading the card?

This can be a real challenge and gets us away from thinking all cards are either-or when really they are ambiguous—can be either positive or negative depending on several circumstances.

This also helps if deciding to use reversals later on, although it does not have to be done using reversals.

ORACLE DECKS

Oracle decks—sometimes referred to as angel cards, medicine cards, or fortune-telling cards—often do not have seventy-eight cards and do not follow four suits and a Major Arcana, but they are just as effective as Tarot cards in guiding or advising us.

The previous sections, dealing with Pips, Courts, and the Major Arcana, will not be helpful in writing interpretations, key words, and such for Oracle decks so I have created a section just for them.

Oracles first came to use in times of Greco-Roman mythology and were deities (or the shrines where they resided) that a priest or priestess would seek out for advice or portents of the future.

Today, oracle is a term that is used to mean a wise or prophetic statement or a source of wisdom.

As a deck of cards they may come in many themes and they are just as effective as fortune-telling cards classified as Tarot cards.

Often Angel cards are used for decks sold in Christian stores or with Christian themes.

Medicine cards often are based on Native American imagery or meanings.

Some Oracle decks might be gods or goddesses, symbols, inanimate objects, all-animals, herbs, household items, or other such categories.

The only thing that really makes a Tarot deck fall into one of these categories is simply that it does not follow the Rider-Waite system with the four elemental suits and the Major Arcana. Some of the cards may not even be numbered.

However, their concept and usage is the same and they are not better or worse then those classified as Tarot, it is all up to an individual's preference and the connection they have to a deck.

I have both Tarot and Oracle decks and I find either one just as easy to work with. Although, the oracle deck I have is a depiction of goddesses so I tend to use that more for one-card readings.

Oracle decks are just as wonderful as Tarot and in some ways they can be better. As I have already stated, typically they have no suits, elements, numerical, or astrological correspondences.

They are used the same as Tarot in that they can be used in spells, meditation, and in readings but in most oracle decks there is no reversed meaning.

Oracle cards also tend to emphasize either only positive points or to voice the negative in a positive way.

For example, a card that basically means you need to find a healthier lifestyle might be phrased this way "a healthy lifestyle brings about positive changes" rather than a doom-n-gloom version like "your bad eating habits will lead to health complications." Both can essentially mean the same thing, but the first is phrased in a more positive way.

Using oracle cards forces a person to be more intuitive because there are no other correspondences.

As I said before in the sections on numerical and elemental correspondences: if you know the element and number meanings then you can read a card without knowing anything else about it.

This can be a bonus because it helps to read decks you are unfamiliar with. An oracle card lacking this may be more difficult to read or remember because you are going on only the imagery.

It may also be easier as well since there are no other associations to try to attach to that card.

Universal VS. Personal Correspondence

What are the universal correspondences for the cards and what are your personal correspondences, do they correlate with each other or do you have other ideas about what the cards mean?

You can try this with just a few random or chosen cards, but eventually you may want to try this with all the cards.

Oracle Card Descriptions

Write/discuss a description for the card based on scenery or imagery only, as if you were describing a picture in a book.

Do not write an interpretation of what the card means, just a description of what you are seeing.

Oracle Key Words

If feeling very ambitious, write a few keywords for every card in the deck but, just as practice you can try writing key words for just a small sample, especially if doing this as a lesson or group activity.

As a long-term project I suggest writing your own key words for each card.

Oracle Key Phrases

As with the idea above, try writing a key phrase or sentence for each of the cards, or if doing this as a lesson or group activity pick a few cards from each suit.

Key phrases can be clichés, a sentence describing the scene, feelings invoked by the scene, etc.

This is a lesson in interpretation and there is no right or wrong, just choose phrases that help you interpret the card.

Oracle Card Interpretations

Using the key words, phrases, and descriptions you have written with the other exercises write your own interpretation for each of the cards in the deck.

Keep these interpretations in a book where you can access them easily and quickly as they may help you in doing readings or can be used as a quick study guide for brushing up on the meanings of the cards.

Random Interpretation

If time or energy does not merit writing an interpretation for all the cards, pick 1-3 at random and write interpretations for them.

This can be done several times until all the cards have been done. If you do this exercise several times and get a card you wrote on previously write a new interpretation for it, and then compare that to the previous one or choose a new card.

Masculine and Feminine Traits

If the cards in an Oracle deck depict people list the masculine and feminine traits that can be associated with it. In cards with no people, such as with an animal deck, are there still masculine or feminine traits that can be seen?

For example, maybe a card with a bear exhibits the qualities of the "momma bear" that protects her young, sometimes fiercely.

Activities or Actions

What activities or actions are taking place in the card?

For example, if a picture of a deity, what are they doing? If a picture of an animal then what is it doing? Sleeping, eating, playing and how does this affect the reading of the card?

If the deck is based on popular media then what are the actions of the characters or the activities in the scene?

All of there were chosen by the creator for a reason, write or discuss possibilities on what these actions may mean.

Mundane and Magical

This exercise uses some knowledge of the Major and Minor Arcana of Tarot, and if unfamiliar with that you can use this book as reference.

Choose five to ten cards first treating it as a Minor Arcana and write or discuss what mundane aspects might be represented in it.

Then, treating it as Major Arcana write or discuss what the spiritual journey or lesson is to be gained from it.

For example, in a card with Sedna, and oceanic Inuit goddess, the spiritual aspect might be accepting oneself as you are or accepting that change is inevitable.

The mundane (Minor Arcana) aspects might be a connection with the seas and animals or a connection to our world.

Think of the spiritual or magical as anything that is intangible and the mundane world as things we can experience with our five senses.

Negative and Positive Traits

Pick five-to-ten cards at random and write/discuss key words or phrases for that card using negative traits or words (grief, despair, regret, etc).

Now, go back and look at those same cards and write or discuss positive traits or words (happiness, success, joy). How do these negative and positive traits work for reading the card?

This can be a real challenge and gets us away from thinking all cards are either-or when really they are ambiguous—can be either positive or negative depending on several circumstances. This also helps if deciding to use reversals later on, although it does not have to be done using reversals.

LEARNING A FEW SPREADS

There are thousands of spreads, sometimes called layouts, for reading cards that use anywhere from one card to twenty or more; most spreads tend to be in a range of three to nine cards.

Readers often find a few spreads they really like but there is no spread better than an another, but certain spreads do work better for certain types of questions.

Have fun trying different spreads' it is fun learning and experimenting with new ones and searching them out on the internet or books. There is literally no end to the number of spreads out there.

Spreads vary in shape and what the positions mean; the shape really has no significance other than to look cool and sometimes the shape looks like the name of the spread (such as the Horseshoe Spread shaped like a horseshoe) but the positions are what carry meaning.

Positions give us a different viewpoint of the card in question. For example, in one spread the position #1 might represent "your self, your conscious mind" whereas in another spread it might mean "the working life, job or career."

Applying this to the card gives each card a different interpretation of its many traits and characteristics.

For example, maybe in the first description the High Priestess shows me that inside I wish to have knowledge, to be open-minded and acquire knowledge on a wide variety of topics and keep records of it.

In the 2nd description the High Priestess may show me that in my working life I either need to use my knowledge to gain a higher position in the work field, or make sure that I give the information only to those who need it.

When trying a new spread do so on your self or on a friend rather than a paying customer. If unfamiliar with it then it can cause your interpretation to be muddled or confused, when reading cards knowing a spread well and how to interpret the positions of it against the meanings in the cards is an important step in the process.

Some spreads may be used for specific questions and others may not.

Spreads like the 'Celtic Cross,' 'Message from the Universe' or a 'Pyramid Spread' can be read without a question in mind and the message will usually just imply a current situation or what a person needs to be aware of in the future. The Year and Week Ahead Spreads are also good for this.

With these spreads the querant doesn't have a question for a certain day or month, they just want to know what that day or month will bring. I also included my favorite spread, the Message from the Universe which is another great spread to do when you do not have a particular question in mind. However, it does require separating all of the cards into their individual suits.

In addition to spreads of a certain number of cards I included the Celtic Cross as it is the most popular spread out there and often one that is seen in the guide books that come with a deck.

I suggest that if you learn or use the Celtic Cross, you should also learn different spreads. I find that nothing is sadder than someone who won't expand their knowledge and learn other spreads.

It's fine if one is your favorite, but by no means feel you have to stick to just one or that you even have to learn the Celtic Cross.

I was in a discussion in a message board once and it seems that people new to Tarot felt they had to learn it and that you aren't a Tarot Reader without knowing it. But, it is an option and not mandatory. It is a good spread, but so are the hundreds of others out there.

Another minor area I want to mention is that some readers lay the cards face-down and then flip them over when all the cards are laid out or as each position is read. Others simply lay them face up as they deal them out (as I do). Neither method is right or wrong.

The only difference between the two styles is that laying the cards face-down, especially if you are flipping them only as each card is read, is that it keeps Querants from trying to read the cards on their own or freaking out over a card such as the Death card before you get around to reading it.

A downfall to this is that you might miss seeing patterns in the spread. When all of them are face up I can read patterns, such as a lot of minors or all pentacles that show up in the spread. But, this can easily be done by just looking for patterns after all the cards have been flipped up.

Learning new spreads is fun and I think it adds an additional challenge; it is helpful to know how to read cards when they fall into different positional meanings or in layouts designed for a different person.

I love looking up spreads in books and the internet to see what other people have come up with and I love seeing ones based on popular media.

Later we will learn how to write your own spreads, which is as addicting as learning new spreads or collecting decks.

Daily Draws

Daily Draws are just that, a card chosen once a day and usually before a person starts their daily routines. A Daily Draw will give a person an idea of what to expect as the day progresses.

Some people express concerns of creating "self-fulfilling prophecies" by seeing a card that depicts woe and hardships setting a person's mind in a negative pessimistic state so that they inadvertently cause the day to be miserable.

I find that I have not had this happen as I usually get so busy I often forget about the card I drew until an event happens or until I go back home and read my journal entry.

There is another way of doing a Daily Draw that will keep self-fulfilling prophecies at bay: pull the card at night after the routines of the day are done.

Focus on the question "what lesson should I have learned today" and read the card accordingly. I find this especially helpful after a tough day that leaves me thinking "why me?" Pulling a Tarot card that same day often brings perspective that we didn't see on our own.

Mysterious Daily Draw

Pick a card randomly, but DO NOT look at it. Instead, just concentrate on the card and write down what you think it is and what images or interpretations you get from it.

Place it somewhere where you can get to it later (do not put it back in the deck).

When you come home write down the day's events.

Now, flip the card over and see if you guessed accurately on both the card and the interpretation.

If not, does the actual card fit with the day's events?

A Month of Daily Draws

One of the challenges I have yet to do for myself is to pull one card every day for a month. Mainly, I just get forgetful and manage only a few days before I lapse.

I do recommend doing this as it is a neat way to get in some practice with the cards as well as observe for any consistencies or patterns.

Yes/No Questions

There are several ways to try and answer Yes/No questions in a Tarot reading but Tarot cards are not really all that accurate for binary questions as Tarot is based on imagery and symbolism and binary questions are an either/or type of thing.

One of the methods I had learned for answering a Yes/No question is to shuffle the deck while thinking of the question, then holding the deck in your hand start flipping cards over.

The Sun represents "Yes" and the Moon is "No." If the Moon card comes up first then the answer is "no" or vice versa.

Another method is to cut the deck after shuffling (and of course thinking of your question) and base the answer on whether it is an odd or an even number. Even numbers would be a "no" and an odd numbers a "yes."

Some questions aren't easily answered in Yes/No fashion but this is a good method to try just as an experiment.

For practice, ask a question in which the answer is already known (to test if the method is accurate) or a question in which the answer can soon be found out like "will I get an interview for the job I applied for?"

The imagery and symbolism of the card can also be used to further interpret the question or situation.

Basic Spread

When just starting out many people use the Celtic Cross as it is in the guidebooks that come with Tarot decks, but often a Past-Present-Future spread or a Basic Spread are included as well.

This is a four-card spread and is very basic and a great starting point for beginners. It can be used for querants who ask a specific question or for those who have no question to ask.

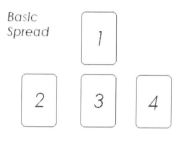

1) WHAT IS AT HAND: the current situation, the need or question the querant has, may even represent the querant. This card can be drawn randomly or a card chosen that represents the querant or situation.

2) PAST INFLUENCES: what is in the querant's past, what led them to this point, what is holding the back or supporting them, what is influencing them or linking them to the past.

3) PONDER THIS: what the querant needs to consider or do in order to continue on and get they outcome they want; how they can achieve the desired outcome or solve the problem at hand.

4) FUTURE INFLUENCE: what they need to be aware of in the future that may affect the outcome either negatively or positively, blocks or obstacles that may occur, something or someone that may aid them in their endeavors, or what the

potential outcome may be.

Three Card Spreads

Three Card spreads are similar in layout to the Basic Spread but omitting the one-card top row.

The most common of the three-card spreads is Past-Present-Future in which three cards are lain down from left to right; the leftmost represents the past, the middle card is the present, and the card on the right is the future.

There are actually hundreds of other three-card (or trinity) spreads and any of them can be used for this prompt. Visit "Know Your Tarot" (www.knowyourtarot.com) for a listing of one-hundred different three-card spreads.

For this prompt I suggest trying to Past-Present-Future Spread first as this is a good one to know to show where a person is at in their life and where they need to be or want to be headed. But try your hand at other three-card spreads as well.

Five Card Spread

Use the basic spread included with this prompt or search online or in books for other five-card spreads and perform one of those.

Record what cards were drawn, your interpretations, and whether the spread seems to work well or not.

As an additional exercise look up other spreads and try one out, compare and contrast it to this basic spread. Which do you like best?

Five Card Spread (position pattern as seen on dice, as a grid, or in a pyramid):

    1) the present or the situation at hand

    2) past influences that are affecting the person or current situations

    3) what the future holds

    4) the reason behind the question or what the querant seeks

    5) the potential outcome.

Seven Card Spread

Use the basic spread included with this prompt or search online or in books for other seven-card spreads and perform one of those.

Record what cards were drawn, your interpretations, and whether the spread seems to work well or not.

As an additional exercise look up other spreads and try one out, compare and contrast it to this basic spread. Which do you like best?

Seven Card Spread (position pattern as seen on dice, as a grid, or in a pyramid):

    1) The present situation

    2) conflicts, challenges, or obstacles obstructing you

    3) changes you need to make to overcome obstacles

    4) your strengths and how they may help you

    5) other challenges or obstacles that may arise

    6) the potential outcome.

Nine Card Spread

Use the basic spread included with this prompt or search online or in books for other nine-card spreads and perform one of those.

Record what cards were drawn, your interpretations, and whether the spread seems to work well or not.

As an additional exercise look up other spreads and try one out, compare and contrast it to this basic spread. Which do you like best?

Nine Card Spread (position pattern as seen on dice, as a grid, or in a pyramid):

1) your querant card

2) your ambitions, desires, or goals

3) what drives you, your motivation

4) your current life path

5) the path you want to be on

6) your weaknesses, addictions, negative traits, or dependencies

7) your strengths, skills, or your positive traits

8) what traits or skills you need to utilize in order to get to where you want to be (spiritually, physically, career, etc)

9) final outcome if you stay on this chosen path.

Message from the Universe Spread

This is my favorite spread as it is useful when I don't know what to ask but feel that there is a message somewhere out there for me. I use it as a personal reading and not for other people as it requires separating all the suits in the deck.

This is time consuming and paying customers don't want to pay for someone to separate a deck, especially if they are paying by the minute, so keep this as.

But, a person could keep a deck just for this purpose and always keep the suits separated, that way there is no valuable time lost by the customer while the reader separates a deck.

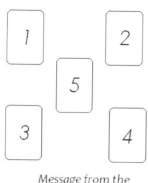

Message from the
Universe Spread

Separate all the suits and the Major Arcana so that there are five separate mini-decks.

Shuffle and cut each of the five decks as if they were separate decks.

For this spread each suit goes in a specific place and not randomly like other spreads.

This is a spread especially good for when the querant has no question and just wants a general reading or needs to clarify their purpose in life.

1) WANDS: this is the working life; jobs or career, manual labors, hobbies, volunteer work.

2) SWORDS: the intellect, internal musings, matters of the mind or lessons to be learned.

3) PENTACLES: the physical life, materialism, basic needs, health, the mundane world.

4) CUPS: the emotional status, all matters of the heart, emotions and feelings.

5) MAJORS: spirituality, internal guidance, spiritual advisors, and the powers that be.

Fan Spread

In an amazing tutorial video by Munisha Khatwani on You Tube I saw this neat spread where the instructor spread all the cards out in a fan and then randomly selected a card, after stating her question.

She continues in this manner asking related questions until she gets a clear view of what she needs to do or what advice is being given.

Let's say the question is "should I apply for the new position at

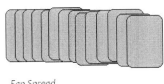

Fan Spread

work." If the card is favorable that yes she should, then another question might be "what skills or strengths do I need to utilize to ensure I get it." A final question might be "will I be happy or successful in that position."

This type of spread is based all on intuition or psychic senses for choosing cards rather than shuffling order and it can be a very effective way to read the cards without being concerned about layouts or attaching meaning to the cards based on positions.

It can also be an easier way to read the cards because we are not trying to compare the card's meaning to that of the position meaning.

The interpretation is based solely on the card and all its symbolism.

Another way to do this without fanning all the cards out is to have the querant cut the deck, then the reader reads the top and bottom card.

Celtic Cross

This is the most popular spread associated with Tarot and the one seen most often in books. I personally do not use it as I feel it is too confusing and I don't really like the meanings/names given to the positions. But, this is just my opinion.

Try it out a few times with yourself or others to see how well it works and whether it is something you want to use.

Often a significator card is chosen; according to A.E. Waite (co-creator of the Rider-Waite system) the courts should be used according to their age categories (more about choosing Querant cards later in this book).

Sometimes the number one spot is the Querant card, sometimes this card is simply set off to the side (as in the example being given here).

According to A.E. Waite the numbers represent the following:

1) what covers the Querant

2) what crosses them

3) what crowns them

4) what is beneath them

5) what is behind them

6) what is before them

7) them self

8) their house

9) their hopes and fears

10) what will come.

There are other options for what these spaces can mean and I recommend going to the link provide in the bibliography of this book for the article by Stefan Stoddard on the website "Tarot Meanings and Readings" to learn more about the Celtic Cross and optional positional meanings.

Pyramid Spread

Pyramid spreads can vary as much a lot as well, and they can be simple with three to seven cards or be complex and use up to twenty or more cards.

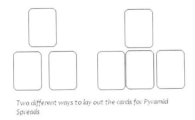

Two different ways to lay out the cards for Pyramid Spreads

Sometimes the positions are used independently like in other spreads and sometimes each row is read as a whole unit (for example, a row might mean "your current situation" and each card in that row identifies with the current situation.)

The most basic Pyramid Spread can be similar to the Past-Present-Future or seen as the Basic Spread already discussed.

We may also see the rows representing something similar to Maslow's Pyramid of Needs where the top row is the self, the 2nd row is our esteem needs (our desire to be recognized or complimented), the 3rd row is our societal needs, the 4th row is our safety needs, and the 5th row is our physiological or physical needs (job, food, shelter) but there are other options as well.

Search the internet or books for some Pyramid Spreads and try a few out, writing or discussing what you like or don't like about it.

Week Ahead Spread

This can be done at any point of the week by simply corresponding the cards and days consecutively.

For example, if doing the reading on a Wednesday then the 1st card will represent Thursday and so on with the last card representing the next Wednesday.

Working people can start this on whatever day is their weekend and get a glimpse of the upcoming work week.

The positions do not mean anything other than the representing the day of the week. It is like a Daily Draw but done a week at a time.

Simply lay the cards out in a row and read each one. Record each card, its interpretation, and then each day record the day's events.

After the week is over review the cards and see if the reading was accurate or write/discuss whether you misinterpreted the card or if your interpretation was different than the reality (such as thinking the 2 of Cups meant your boyfriend would propose but instead what happened is your boss offered you a partnership with the company you work for).

Year Ahead Spread

Do a reading for each day of the upcoming year. This can be done on the 1st day of the New Year (or close to it) by laying out 12 cards at once, reading each one for the months consecutively (try four rows of three starting left to right with the #1 spot being January).

Or, you can spend the next twelve days pulling one card every day with each day and card representing a month.

In the Pacific Islands there is a belief that how you live the first 12 days of the year is how the remaining year will play out, so I created the above method based on that concept.

Record each card, the month it represents, and the interpretation.

Then, at the end of each month summarize the entire month and relate that back to the card's interpretation to see how accurate it was or if there is some new insight to be gained from the card.

For example, perhaps the Hermit card was interpreted as spending that month alone or lonely but then after the month is over and you look back and realize "hey, I started college this month" then the Hermit will be re-interpreted as seeking knowledge.

Sometimes we misread cards based on our emotions or distractions at the time, but if we look back on the cards later we can gain new insight.

Birthday Spread

This spread is one I created and I have done several of them for friends as well as doing one for myself each year.

It should be done on the person's birthday or close to it as possible. Though this spread was written by me there are other versions of birthday spreads out there.

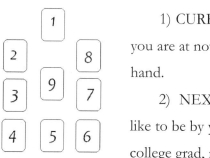

1) CURRENT SITUATION: where you are at now in your life or what is at hand.

2) NEXT YEAR: where you would like to be by your next   birthday (i.e., college grad, married)

3) EMPOWERMENT: what empowers or motivates you, your inspirations, muses and heroes.

4) GOALS: what you need to do or create to bring you closer to your goals.

5) MATERIAL STATE: where you are at physically and financially.

6) EMOTIONAL STATE: where you are emotionally or what is driving/hindering your goals.

7) SPIRITUAL STATE: what motivates you spiritually or where you are at on a spiritual level.

8) OBSTACLES: what stands in opposition to your objective; obstacles, internal fears, doubts.

9) ACTION: what you need to do to make your dreams or goals become fulfilled.

Group or Club Readings

Reading for a group or club is always interesting, I did this for the Tarot group we had and it went very well in that it was accurate and people all added their two-cents worth.

This can give real insight as to how a group is viewed by nonmembers and in what direction it needs to go to achieve its desired results.

1) PURPOSE: what is the group's purpose or mission?

2) FUTURE: what is the future of the group?

3) DRIVING FORCE: what motivates or inspires the group, what keeps it going day to day.

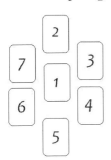

4) SERVICE: how the group can serve the community or other group members.

5) FOCUS: what does the group need to focus on more.

6) TOOLS: what tools or knowledge does the group need to maintain its status or grow.

7) COMMUNITY VIEWS: how does the community view the group as a whole?

Try Different Layouts

Over the course of a month choose three to five different layouts and try them out either on your self or for friends.

Write/discuss how well they worked, did you like it (why or why not) and how it could be improved or changed.

Compare Layouts

Pick two or three different layouts. Pick a position in the layouts and compare how the meaning of a randomly chosen card changes based on the position.

For example, if having a Past-Present-Future Spread, Celtic

Cross, or Universal spreads look at the #2 spot in each one which would be: the present, what is crossing you, the Intellect.

Now, draw a card. Let's say it is the Two of Cups. How does the meaning of this card change based on the various layouts?

Learn Three Layouts Well

At some point you may not have access to a plethora of different spreads. For instances such as these, learn three basic spreads very well so that you can use them whenever you are asked to do a reading.

I recommend a three-card spread, the Universal Message spread and at least one other non-topic specific spread so that you have a decent "arsenal" of spreads to use whether you have access to books, your notes, or the internet.

Still, it is a good idea to keep a variety of spreads on hand at all times such as kept in your Tarot Kit or wherever you store your cards so that you have more than just three in which to choose from.

Sometimes Querants want to know about a specific topic such as career or romance and you can look through your notes or a book and choose a spread that fits.

PATTERNS IN READINGS

Now that you have tried a few spreads, it is time to do readings and pay attention to patterns that emerge as these are every bit as important as the card's meanings.

For example, a lack of minor cards means the resolutions relies on spiritual or divine guidance, whereas a reading mostly of minors means it will be a quick and mundane resolution.

Numbers missing from a reading, elements that repeat, dominate or missing…all of these can influence the meaning of the reading.

When we read the cards we need to look at all aspects of it, if the artist drew it in there it has significance.

Look at the card's meaning in relation to the position it is in (is it a past card, or does the position mean work life, etc).

Then, look at the color choices, elements, numbers, etc. Look at the cards in relation to each other. As stated in the past paragraph, are they all of the Minor Arcana? Maybe there is a numerical sequence such as 1, 2, 3, 4 or maybe a card lacking from that such as 1, 2, 4, 5. What would this mean to the reading?

In the next readings you do, look for these different patterns in order to gain a better understanding of the cards, their meanings, and the situation at hand.

As part of a "checklist" I had created for myself I wrote down what types of things to look at in cards such as the elements, numbers, and the amount of Majors and Minors.

It can be essential to a reading and if you are getting "Tarot Readers' Block" and cannot draw any interpretations based on the card itself, there is a lot to be gained by using just the elemental, numerical, and symbolic correspondences.

Elemental Patterns

Do a reading of five or more cards and look for patterns: check for elemental patterns such as more than one element, an even amount, etc.

Write down the patterns you see and what this means for the reading (without reading the cards or their positions).

Numerical Significance or Patterns

Do a reading of five or more cards and look for patterns: look for numerical patterns such as repeated numbers, sequential numbers, or odd versus even.

Write down the patterns you see and what this means for the reading (without reading the cards or their positions).

Zodiac Patterns

I suggest familiarizing yourself with the symbols of the Zodiacs and their imagery (such as a crab for Cancer and so on) in order to recognize them in a Tarot card.

Even if these are written down and kept with your decks or Tarot notes it is helpful in interpreting the cards and for those not used to working with astrology some of the people, objects or animals seen in a card we may not automatically associate with a Zodiac sign.

In a reading look for these items and write or discuss how they aid in the reading or what they might mean.

Look for Major vs. Minor significance

Do a reading of five or more cards and look for patterns: look at the number of majors versus the number of minors in the deck.

Write down the patterns you see and what this means for the reading (without reading the cards or their positions).

In Oracle decks, look for other patterns such as more domestic or tame animals than wild (could mean the answer is close to home) or in decks of deities look for the number of females to males, etc.

Typically, a lot or mostly minors in a reading means the answer is mundane and simple and a lot or all Majors means that the answer will be achieved through spiritual guidance or divine intervention.

What's Missing

When reading for patterns, it is important to notice what is missing from the pattern as this can indicate what is missing from the person's life and perhaps what they need to do in order to achieve their desired results.

For example, three of the elements show up multiple times but there is no suit of pentacles. If the person asked a question such as "when will I see financial security or success?" the problem might be in that they are not paying attention to their finances.

Either they are not working, need a higher-paying job, or are not spending their money wisely. Or perhaps only minors are present which could mean a person needs to look for spiritual guidance or within them selves.

Do a reading of five to seven cards and write or discuss what is missing from the pattern.

Connecting Patterns

First, read just the basic or universal message as conveyed in the guidebooks and then tie this into the numerical, symbolic and elemental correspondences as well as the position the card is in the layout in order to get a complete interpretation of the card.

Think of it as a formula: Basic Meaning + Numerical Meaning + Meaning of Symbols + Elemental Meaning + Position = Total Interpretation.

One Reading; Two Decks

Take two different decks. Ask the question of one deck and set it up in a layout. Ask the same question (worded exactly the same) of the second deck and lay it out in the same pattern.

Record any similarities or differences, write which reading is more accurate, or if they both are then write what the major components are that you got out of each reading.

Look to see if there are similar patterns such as numbers or elements missing from the reading or the same number of Major Arcana, etc.

Practice Readings

In order to gain confidence and be proficient in reading cards people need to practice. If we pull their cards out once a year, dust them off, and head to the local fair or festival to read we are not as likely to be as good as the person who uses cards almost daily.

But if there is no one to read for what is a person supposed to do? Granted, there is always the option of doing a self-reading but sometimes that isn't necessary or merited.

In order to gain practice try reading for different situations or "intangible" people such as fictional characters or celebrities—that is, people we don't know personally.

This gives us practice at interpreting the cards and using all the knowledge gained thus far (looking for symbols, patterns, interpreting card based against its position in the layout, etc) and gives us practice at setting up our performance.

During your practice readings you may notice that you needed an extra card or had a card fall out while shuffling. There are "extra" cards that can come up randomly or be drawn on purpose in a reading.

Bonus cards adds something to the reading, a wild card is one that falls from deck on its own when shuffling or laying out the cards, and clarification cards clear up a confusing read or answer.

They may not be necessary in every reading but keep in mind prompts at the end of this segment in case they do come up.

Read for a Pet

Do a reading for a pet you have or have had in the past. Does the reading fit the personality quirks of your pet?

Animals also have different elemental correspondences based on habitat (fish and amphibians are water, mammals are earth, birds are air, and lizards or spiders are fire, etc) did elemental patterns show up that correlate with your animal's habitat?

For example, did an Earth cards come up for a reading you did on your cat?

Fictional Characters

Pick a TV, movie or book character that you know very well and do a reading for them as if they were a real person sitting across from you.

Did the reading come out accurate for the events that occur to them in the book, TV show or movie?

I did one for the character Rose on James Cameron's 1996 "Titanic." I got a card depicting choices needed to be made, which is exactly what she did when she chose Jack over Cal.

You can also perform a reading for a fairy tale character such as Red Riding Hood, Snow White or Sleeping Beauty.

Celebrity Readings

While its not ethical to do readings on people that haven't asked for one, reading for a celebrity for practice is not going to harm anyone in that we may never know if the information is correct (not like peeking into your neighbor to see if her husband is cheating) and we will unlikely run across that person ever. Just don't put your results on the internet.

Does the reading fit with current news about the celebrity or fit with their celebrity status (rich, gives to charity, entrepreneur, actor, musician?)

Read for Yourself

Pick either a situation that has already happened and do a spread of choice (Universal Message works great for past events) to see what lesson should have been learned.

Or, pick a future event and do a reading for it. Pick something that will or should happen soon so that when it does you can test your interpretation skills and see if you accurately depicted the outcome.

Reading for a Business

Do a reading to get the general atmosphere of a business. Does it fit with the general atmosphere of the business?

For example, if a family restaurant did you get a card that symbolizes family?

Use this reading for a business that you know well so you can determine if the reading fits with the business, for example is it family-oriented or does it fit with the type of business (bank, museum, restaurant.)

Geographical Reading

Do readings to get the general atmosphere geographical place, such as the town you live in. Does it fit with the general atmosphere or culture of the area?

For example, if there is a military base there did you get a military inspired card such has a King or Knight? If the town is known as a tourist town did you get a card indicating travel or outsiders?

How about a college town? Did a card come up indicating education or knowledge?

Sports Outcomes or Dynamics

For a sports event that is coming up do a reading to see if you can get the results or outcome of the event. Keep track of the event and compare to your reading to see if you were right.

Current or Past Event

Perform a reading for a current or past event and see what the cards tell you about it. Is it an accurate description? A tragic event might show the Tower Card which indicates major upheaval to the point of verging on catastrophe.

Like the previous entry, a reading like this gives you good practice because it is something you already know about and will soon find out about (if a current event) and this helps a reader build confidence in interpreting the cards.

Read with a Non-Tarot Deck

It can be rewarding and a fun challenge to try and read with a non-Tarot card deck. Poker decks can be read, and my daughter did a reading with her Pokémon cards.

Cards with images or different people such as Old Maid or Go Fish would be fun to try as well. Don't take a reading too seriously this way, it is just for practice and just to give your brain and intuition some exercise.

Critique Your Own Reading

Critique a reading you did for yourself—do you feel it was accurate, where there cards or meanings you stumbled over?

You may want to wait 24-hours before critiquing your own reading as a slight separation from it can give more insight.

Write down all feelings and interpretations and cards, then come back a day later and critique.

Readings with only Majors or Minors

Separate all of the Major Arcana out of the deck and do a

reading using just the majors.

Record the layout and interpretations of the reading and discuss or write if this reading worked, how was it to use just the majors, etc.

Try also using just majors and aces or just majors and court cards.

Then, read with minors only, does the reading lack something when either set is omitted or does the reading still work for the situation?

Perform 10 Readings (without using a book)

Hopefully readers will come to a point where they will read cards without a book hardly at all, if ever, but until a person gains confidence in reading cards without some assistance make it a personal goal to do at least ten different readings without looking in book.

Gaining confidence at reading the cards based on my own intuition was something I struggled with and had to learn and, ultimately, the birthing idea of this book.

So, to read ten layouts without looking at a book gave me confidence and eventually the majority of readings I did on my self or others was done without referencing any books or notes.

Clarification Cards

When doing a reading that is unclear draw an extra card from the deck. It can either apply to the whole reading or just a particular card. A clarification card can also be used for advice.

Say, for example, the reading says to look for a new career, if the clarification card is a Seven of Pentacles it may indicate that the person needs to look at a career that involves their own skills (writing, organizing, art, etc).

Using a clarification card may not always be necessary but use it in some practice readings to get a feel for how to interpret a card as such.

Bonus Cards

Bonus cards can also help to clarify a meaning but can also be used to show an alternate outcome, or a future outcome.

After doing a reading pull another card to see what the outcome would be if a person chooses a different path or ask how they can change the outcome predicted in the reading.

This isn't really clarifying a confusing reading or card but adding something extra to the reading that wasn't originally revealed.

Bottom of the Deck

At the end of a reading turn the deck over and read the bottom card, this is a card that reveals a hidden meaning or secret that was not revealed in the regular layout.

This could be a secret someone is keeping from the querant, something the querant is refusing to acknowledge, inner turmoil or conflictions, or anything hidden in the subconscious or being ignored or repressed.

Wild Cards

Often when shuffling or laying out a card one will fall from the deck. I was told early on, when this happened to me, to "quick, grab it and read it!" When I did it accurately depicted acts of creativity and success with it (I was working on my first book then).

If one (or even a few) cards fall while shuffling or laying out a spread these are the universe's way of saying "here's something else I want you to know."

Read those cards in addition to whatever cards are in the spread. However, sometimes we really fumble and may lose half the deck, don't try to read them all! Simply pick them back up and reshuffle.

REVERSALS

One of the most common misconceptions is that reversals are an absolute must in a Tarot reading. I used to be guilty of thinking this as well because I believed that all cards had a positive meaning when upright and all cards reversed were negative.

This, however, is not the case—not even remotely close. Each card can denote both positive and negative aspects depending on the question, how the person reads it, and the position's meaning in the spread.

Let's take the Fool as an example this time: in one way he is on a new journey, full of hopes and dreams and promises; but in a different light he is not heeding the warnings given to him and he is not looking where he is going (off the edge of a cliff) and heading for danger.

There are some cards that are more ambiguous than others and tend to be have a more negative meaning than other cards, for example the Sun card is usually happiness, success, things going your way and the Ten of Swords is despair or a grim outcome as the person is facedown on the floor with swords poking out of his back.

But even these can have opposite meanings such as the sun being over-optimistic and blinded to the situation and the Ten of Swords can indicate the worst is over; things can only get better from here.

And none of these are looked at in the reverse, just depending on how they end up in a reading. Of course, if reversed they do add meaning to a spread in much the same ways I just did above.

Sometimes a reversed card is just the exact opposite of the upright meaning but this isn't always the case. With reversals it is important to pay attention to what the images or scene on the card conveys and how they look reversed.

For example, in the Tower the people are jumping out of the building and falling. But when reversed they are ascending rather than descending.

Also in the Tower the people may be falling head first, which is going to be a bad landing but when reversed they are positioned feet first, meaning they are in the right position for good things to happen.

If a reversal comes up in a reading it could also mean that a message is being blocked either consciously or unconsciously (something is keeping the reader from seeing the answer or moving forward).

It could also mean that a situation is delayed, postponed, cancelled, or that something has already happened and is not yet accepted or understood.

Reversals can also show the shadow side of an issue, a darker or secretive side to a person, unspoken or unacknowledged issues, weaknesses, or perhaps strengths that are being ignored or misused.

Reversals may show an unconscious defense mechanism that is propelling us to cast out negativity or block our own efforts. Cards in the reversed position could also mean a sudden, unexpected or unwanted change in direction or situation.

A reversed Court Card may either mean the opposite gender of the person depicted or a person with the negative traits assigned to that card. Perhaps it means a person who is giving bad advice in order to further their own means or is misusing their skills and knowledge.

Reversals can also mean time is wasted, skills are being misused; a past event has not been dealt with or accepted; messages are not understood, are blocked or ignored; or a situation is being delayed.

Reading a reversal takes the same intuitiveness that reading uprights does and there are many variables to the meaning of the card. Most books sold on Tarot, including the tiny guidebooks sold with decks, will list the meanings for reversals. Just remember, it is the choice of the reader and not the querant to use reversals.

To add in reversals lay the deck down on a large flat surface such as a table, and then spread it out. Keep swirling and mixing the cards until there is a haphazard pile on the table. Bring them all back together again and stack in a deck.

Another method is to hold the deck in your hand and cut, turn the top portion 180 degrees and place it back on top. Cut the deck again at a different level and repeat. Continue this process until an adequate amount of reversals have been added to the deck.

In reading reversals only the meanings of the card changes, the numerical and elemental correspondences do not change.

For example: a card depicting a cup that is having water poured into it indicate an influx of emotions, but when reversed the water will look as it is pouring out which could mean you are devoid or empty of emotions. The water element still means emotions, but whether the "cup is half full or half empty" depends on which way the card faces.

Remember: using reversals is a personal choice of the reader, not the querant. Let me recommend however, that if you choose to use reversals then make sure you mix it up occasionally.

If you create reversals, and then store the deck in a box and each and every time you pick the deck back up it is held in the same way then certain cards will *always be reversed* and you will never get their upright meaning.

Each time you do a reading cut the deck and reverse the cards randomly so that it is different reversals each and every time or lay them all out on a table, spreading them haphazardly, and then pick them back up as a means of shuffling so that you can be assured different cards end up as reversals each time.

Reversal Importance and Significance

What is the significance of having (or not having) reversals in a deck? Do you think reverse meanings are essential to Tarot or

Oracle decks? Why or why not? Do you think reversals enhance or diminish the meaning of the layouts?

Universal VS Personal Correspondences

What are the universal correspondences for the pips and what are your personal correspondences, do they correlate with each other or do you have other ideas about what the cards mean?

You can try this with just a few random or chosen cards, but eventually you may want to try this with all the cards.

Reversals Descriptions

Write/discuss a description for each of the cards based on scenery or imagery only, as if you were describing a picture in a book. Do not write an interpretation of what the card means, just a description of what you are seeing. How do the scenes change from your original scene or card descriptions with the uprights?

Reversal Key Words

If feeling very ambitious, write a few keywords for every card in the deck in their reversed form. But, just as practice you can try writing key words for just a small sample, especially if doing this as a lesson or group activity.

Pick two to three cards from each suit, including the Major Arcana. However, if you plan on using reversals I suggest writing your own key words for each card. Sit with your deck and pull out all of the same number in the suits, such as all the Aces, and write key words for them. Continue until all the suits are done and then write for the Major Arcana by selecting a few cards each day.

Reversal Key Phrases

As with the idea above, try writing a key phrase or sentence for each of the reversed cards, or if doing this as a lesson or group activity pick a few cards from each suit.

Key phrases can be clichés, a sentence describing the scene, feelings invoked by the scene, etc. This is a lesson in interpretation and there is no right or wrong, just choose phrases that help you interpret the card.

Reversal Interpretations

Using the key words, phrases, and descriptions you have written with the other exercises write your own interpretation for each of the reversed cards in the deck.

Keep these interpretations in a book where you can access them easily and quickly as they may help you in doing readings or can be used as a quick study guide for brushing up on the meanings of the cards.

Random Interpretation

If time or energy does not merit writing an interpretation for all the reversed cards, pick 1-3 at random and write interpretations for them.

This can be done several times until all the cards have been done. If you do this exercise several times and get a card you wrote on previously write a new interpretation for it, and then compare that to the previous one or choose a new card.

Practice Reading

Shuffle the cards so you get a decent mix of reversed and uprights.

Choose a topic for a reading to do on your self and perform it using both reversals and uprights.

Compare and contrast this to other readings you have done, do you like it better or not? Did using reversals add to the meaning? Do you feel the meaning or reading was accurate or was it just more confusing?

All Reverse Practice Reading

I don't really know anyone who reads using only reversals, although my daughter did try it one time and came up with an accurate reading. It is still good practice and would be interesting to try out. Reverse the entire deck and perform a reading.

Consider the following questions: Did it work? Why or why not? Was there still a mix of positive and negative meanings in the reading? Do you think the reading was accurate?

Negative and Positive Traits

Pick five-to-ten cards at random and write/discuss key words or phrases for the card in its reverse position using negative traits or words (grief, despair, regret, etc). Now, go back and look at those same cards and write or discuss positive traits or words (happiness, success, joy).

How do these negative and positive traits work for reading the card? This can be a real challenge and gets us away from thinking all cards are either-or when really they are ambiguous—can be either positive or negative depending on several circumstances.

Querant, Power, or Significator Cards

Whether it is called a querant card, power card or significator card, adding one to your readings can be a useful tool. It can help the querant see the situation differently or see their role in the situation.

A card of this manner can be chosen in one of several ways (as seen in the prompts below) and either becomes part of the reading and used in conjunction with the other cards or used as a sort of focal point for the reading in which it summarizes the person or their situation.

There are different ways you can determine a personal card and there is no "right or wrong" method for doing so. Also, querant cards are an option of the reader as well.

It can aid in a reading by adding insights about the person receiving the reading and to help keep the reading focused on the querant. A querant card can also be used in conjunction with the other cards in the spread.

For example, a reader will look at the personality traits of the querant card and use that to determine how they would respond or react to the situations presented in the main spread.

The following methods can be used to choose cards either for your self or for others but for these prompts choose cards for yourself for the practice of using a querant card in a reading. It is no good to try and figure out how to use these additional cards while you are reading for someone.

Remember: practice makes perfect and this book's main focus is about becoming confident in reading the cards before trying them out on others.

Date of Birth Method

Find your power or querant card based on your birth date. Add up all the numbers and if greater than 21 reduce it to a single digit. For example 04-25-1978 would be $4+2+5+1+9+7+8=36$.

If the total is a single digit, or a number between ten and twenty-one then do nothing further.

But, since the Major arcane does not go higher than twenty-one any numbers higher than that, as in the example above, must be reduced to a single digit such as $3+6=9$.

Date of Birth Method—Compared to Minors

Compare your number with the cards in the other suits.

For example, if you got a four as your card look at the fours in the other suits and see if they compare or contrast to your power card and if they also fit in with your life.

Male / Female Method

I have seen a generic method of using Male-Female genders to determine a querant card simply by using the Magician for males and the High Priestess for females.

However, this may not always be accurate as not everyone fits in with the characteristics of those cards. Also, the cards depict archetypal qualities of people so even though the Magician is often depicted as male I might identify more with the traits of that card rather than that of the High Priestess.

So, for this prompt, pull all the cards in the Major Arcana with a person on them, look at all the male cards and choose one that fits you the best, then look at all the females and choose one that fits you the best.

Now, out of those two cards spend sometime writing, discussing or just thinking about the traits they have and determine which one fits you the best. Remember, as a female you might connect more with a male card, and vice versa.

Zodiacal Method

Power cards can be chosen based on the Zodiac. Wands are the signs of Aries, Leo, and Sagittarius; Cups is Cancer, Scorpio, and Pieces; Swords are Gemini, Libra, and Aquarius; and Pentacles are Taurus, Virgo, and Capricorn.

Combine this with the Birth date method to choose your card in that suit. For example, if your birth date number is five and your zodiac sign is Swords then that is your querant card. Write or discuss whether you think it fits your personality or not.

Court Appearance Method

Some use different suits to depict different appearances or characteristic types. This can be a good way to determine a querant card but involves the court cards only.

Wands would be for people that are paler skin, blue eyes, and blonde or light-colored hair.

Cups are for people with light to medium skin tones, brown hair, and green or hazel eyes.

Swords are anyone with an olive skin tone, dark hair, and any light colored eyes.

Pentacles are people with dark skin, dark hair, and dark eyes.

This does not refer to races as there are different shades of people in all races, so use your best judgment.

Write or discuss your feelings on this method and if you think it is accurate.

Court Appearance Based on Age

After determining your court suit based on the above method you can decide on which court card of that suit you are based on age.

Pages and knights are typically youthful, up to about age twenty-five with pages being female and knights being male (although this restriction is loose and can be either/or).

Queens are mature women and Kings are mature men. However, remember that a twenty-year old might be more mature than others of their same age and might identify more with a Queen card.

Age can be determined physically or mentally and emotionally.

Determine which card fits you best and write or discuss which card you are and why, or write and discuss why you do not fit with one of your chronological age if that is the case.

Court Appearance Based on Personality

You can also look at the four court cards and determine if you are the:

1) Page (a messenger, go-to person, always doing what others say);

2) Knight (chivalrous, a hero, a go-getter, always in the mix of the excitement)

3) Queen (matronly, stands beside her King but can be a ruler as well, cares for people)

4) or a King (a ruler, likes order over chaos, disciplinarian).

Remember, a man can be a Queen and a female can be a King and Pages and Knights are neutral genders.

Don't forget to look at the meaning of the suit and see if it fits as well.

Emotions Method

You can choose a card based on the emotions or typical personality of the person.

Wands would be people are passionate and energetic.

Cups are for those that are emotional and creative.

Swords consider themselves intellectual and logical.

Pentacles are practical people.

Personal Choice

Another method is to simply sift through all the cards and choose one that you most identify with.

This is good for others to do when reading for them as well as it gives the reader insight into how the querant views them selves and places their energies on the card.

If you do this for yourself, write or discuss why you chose this card. If someone else chose it for them selves and you did a reading write or discuss how this helped you in reading for that person.

Combine Them All

Combine the different cards you got from each of the methods. What are the similarities and differences? Do they all fit with some aspect of your life?

For example, I am the High Priestess (birth date) and Swords (court method) and Cups (Zodiac) and all three fit me. I am knowledgeable but give that knowledge out when needed, I am a communicator (writer), and I am emotional.

Preferred Method

Having tried the various methods of choosing a querant card, write or discuss which is your preferred method and why?

Use in a Reading for Yourself

Now that you have determined your querant card, regardless of what method you used, place it in a reading and discuss whether it worked for you or the reading or not.

How does the card (i.e., your personality) correspond to the reading or interact with the other cards.

Use in a Reading for Others

Use your preferred method to use a Querant card for someone else's reading.

Consider the following questions: was it easy to choose a card? Did you benefit from using the Querant card? Do you think the querant benefited from it?

WRITING SPREADS

Creating spreads, I have found, is spreads is a very fun, creative, and addictive exercise. It also takes a certain level of skill and creativity to create spreads and positions that will work in a Tarot reading and be applicable when reading the cards.

I don't remember the first time I tried to write a spread or even what prompted me to do so, but I do remember how excited I was when it worked well and I do know that it can become quite addicting to create spreads.

Every Tarot reader should attempt to write at least one, just for the experience of it.

To write a spread, the first thing to do is consider its purpose.

That is, what is it that you want the spread to achieve or what do you want to know about? Is it for love or financial matters? Will the spread be used for general and not specific purposes? Having a purpose helps to formulate the actual spread.

Next, consider the theme of the spread. Spreads can be based on a theme (movies or pop culture), on holidays, or on concepts (luck, love, decision-making).

Having a theme can help tie everything together and helps to organize the spread. Do you want a theme of a movie or television show? Maybe you want to use all of the suits like in the Message from the Universe spread?

A theme can also be a simple three-card spread but with your own positions instead of the basic past, present, future concept.

Then, think of positions that fit with that theme but also coincide with the purpose of the deck.

There is no use in having a position that indicates "career or job" in a spread meant only for romance. Positions should be based on the theme as well, such as the Halloween spread I created a couple of years ago.

Some of the positions I used, based on stereotypical Halloween "monsters", are: ghost, your spiritual side; witch, your magical side; Frankenstein, the physical aspects; werewolf, our base and primal needs; vampire, are sensual and sexual side; and mummy, what we keep under wraps.

Finally, give the spread a name and try it out, tweaking any areas necessary in order to make it work well. Perform some practice readings to see what works and what doesn't.

Here is an example of creating a Tarot spread:

I want a spread that is for general purposes and I want it based on the television show "Destination Truth" on the Syfy channel. It will by a spread to determine the greater truth or enlightenment. "Destination Truth" is a television show hosted by Josh Gates in which he and his crew travel to exotic places in search of ghosts, supernatural entities or cryptids.

I have my purpose and theme so now I need to create positions. I can either use categories of the creatures they seek: underground or cave dwellers, spirits, tree dwellers, water beings, air creatures, and land animals.

Perhaps spirits deal with the inner self, my spirituality; underground or cave dwellers are my secret self, the part of me no one sees or knows of; tree dwellers might be my intellectual self; air creatures are my thoughts, inspiration and creativity; water beings are the emotional side and terra creatures are the physical self (my health, finances, etc).

I can go with a different theme as well and try for the crew members: the leader, the medic, tech experts, or investigators. The leader is just that, leadership qualities or success, where I am headed in life; the medic is my personal health and well-being; the tech expert is my intellectual self; and the female is the feminine qualities or motherly instincts.

As a bonus card I can toss in an extra: the translator. When the team visits foreign countries they usually enlist the aid of a language translator. In my spread, the translator could be a clarification card or even a card indicating how the world sees me or how I see the world.

The form of the Tarot Spread can also be included and while there is no real purpose to it, it does add aesthetic appeal. For example, a Tarot spread for love might have the cards laid out in the form of a heart or a spread to show areas of strengths or weaknesses in the chakra might be laid out in an arc like a rainbow.

Some spreads are simply the cards lined up in a row or a basic grid. There might not even be a layout, for example, a person might simply state what the card represents (past, present, future, etc) and then draw the cards one at a time.

In my experiences there are five basic spread formats: circles (to show cycles); grids or straight rows to show a series of events; steps or pyramids to show either advancing, progression, or building on something; and horseshoe shapes to indicate paths diverging or choices.

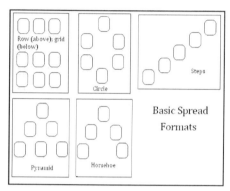

Aside from that, people can make up their own shapes to spreads as well. I have seen ones in shapes of hearts, stars, and all sorts of other geometric patterns.

Half the fun of creating your own spreads is the creativity that can go into each one, so don't let basic spread formats hold you back from inventing your own or get into a rut thinking you have to use only the spreads you see in books or the internet.

Write Your Own Basic Spread

This can be combined with either a three-card spread or a five-card spread or try using a four-card spread as discussed earlier. However many cards used, create a basic spread that can be used quickly and for general questions or readings (when the querant has no specific question in mind).

Write Your Own Three Card Spread

Write a spread using three cards, make sure you indicate what the positions mean. Three card spreads can be designed in horizontal, vertical, or diagonal lines or as a pyramid (one card on top and two on the bottom).

Write Your Own Five Card Spread

Write a spread using five cards, make sure you indicate what the positions mean, give it a shape, and finally give your spread a name.

Write Your Own Seven Card Spread

Write a spread using seven cards, make sure you indicate what the positions mean, give it a shape, and finally give your spread a name.

Write Your Own Nine Card Spread

Write a spread using nine cards, make sure you indicate what the positions mean, give it a shape, and finally give your spread a name

Write Your Own Birthday Spread

Write your own birthday spread, make sure you indicate what the positions mean and give the spread a shape and a name. It can be with as many cards as desired or try writing a few different spreads using different numbers of cards.

Write Your Own Group Spread

Write your own group spread, make sure you indicate what the positions mean and give the spread a shape and a name. It can be with as many cards as desired or try writing a few different spreads using different numbers of cards. If you are not involved in any groups do the spread for a family.

Write Your Own Two-Person Spread

Write your own two-person spread, make sure you indicate what the positions mean and give the spread a shape and a name. It can be with as many cards as desired or try writing a few different spreads using different numbers of cards.

Write Your Own Spread of Your Choice

A free-for-all to write a spread of any type desired. Writing spreads are addicting and sometimes we have a topic in mind (a romance spread) or just a shape (a heart). Think of a topic of shape that you'd like to see and create a spread for it.

Write a Spread on Specific Topic

Writing spreads for specific topics is tricky, each position should be indicative of the topic. For example, if doing a romance spread it doesn't make sense to have one of the positions be "financial matters, what motivates you financially" but having a position of "what you are looking for in a partner" does make sense.

Write a spread on a specific topic and have the positions

matched up to the topic. This can be with any number of cards. Often when spreads are on a specific topic they also are shaped as such, like cards lain out in a heart shape.

Write Your Own Holiday Spread

Holiday spreads are the most fun as they can take on a variety of shapes and the meaning or names for the positions is limitless.

Pick a favorite holiday and write a spread for it.

For example, my daughter and I wrote a spread for Groundhog's Day in which we had three cards on the bottom row to represent the ground (what grounds us, keeps us stable) with one card on the top row to indicate the groundhog coming out of the hole and our self or current situation.

Then we laid a card on top of the groundhog card as his shadow, and this indicated what was overshadowing us, what we were afraid of, or what inhibited us.

Write Your Own Spread Based on Popular Media

Basing spreads on popular media is a lot of fun and there are innumerable spreads on the internet that do so.

I have seen spreads for Titanic, American Idol and Buffy the Vampire Slayer, just to name a few.

Pick a favorite movie, concept, or television show and write a spread based on the concept of the show or the characters in it. Each position can be named for a specific character and their qualities or personality is the basis for the meaning.

For example, a character that is well-organized the position named for them might mean "being orderly, adverse to chaos, what needs to be in place or in order."

Write Your Own Pyramid Spread

Pyramid Spreads can be on any topic at all and can be simple three-card spreads but most tend to be five to nine cards and you can always use more cards too.

Each card can have its own meaning in the spread or you can denote meanings to the rows. For example, in a spread with three rows, the first row can represent the past, middle row is the present, and bottom row is the future.

Or, you can go "up" the spread and start with the bottom row it can mean the basic situation, middle row is where you are at now, and top row is where you want to be.

What Do You Like Best?

Now that you have gotten some experience at writing spreads, what do you like best about them? Have you found that you can write good spreads, are they easy for you to do, and how well do they work in a reading? Are there some that didn't work so well?

What Do You Like Least?

What do you like the least? In what areas are you having difficulty writing a spread (the shape, the focus, the positions)? Are they not working well with the cards, are they confusing, do your querant's not like them? Write or discuss everything that you dislike about writing spreads.

Develop a Performance

One of the things I learned that was really valuable to me, aside from reading the cards, was how to develop a performance. We learn how to read cards when we study Tarot but then we have to learn *how* to read the cards as in how do we project that information to others.

If doing readings for other people they are going to expect something unique and memorable and the ambience is as important as the meaning in the cards. Give people what they came for (whether paying or not) so that they will come back for more readings, especially if this becomes a paid business.

Developing a performance might sound like we're doing a sideshow act, but that isn't the case here.

A performance sets the mood of both the reader and the querant to be of a receptive mind to see and hear the messages conveyed.

It also can cleanse the space to be free of negativity and create an aura or atmosphere for a reading done well instead of haphazard and sloppy.

A performance shows other people that you care about the

cards, the art form, the act and the experience of Tarot and can lend a professional feel that makes the querant comfortable and confident.

Creating a performance is not a show, it is not something that should be done with strobe lights, loud music, and dancing monkeys.

But think of it this way: if you walk into a massage therapist office do you want to just be shoved into a room, told to undress and then lay on a cold table with an uncaring masseuse?

Or, it is better if the masseuse explains the process, turns the lights down low, has the room temperature at a comfortable level, and uses oils or lotions?

Creating a performance for the person needing a reading is providing them with a comfortable and rewarding experience.

Performances or 'rituals' for reading the cards can be done on a personal level as well such as always reciting a blessing before doing a reading, or maybe listening to soft music and lighting candles.

Don't forget that you are important as well, and you can create an ambience for yourself when reading.

Now, this isn't always necessary (I quite often just perform a simple reading on my couch while the kids watch TV or play on the computer) but creating a performance for yourself is a small way to pamper yourself and get quiet or relaxation time.

One thing to consider as well when reading for others is to not sugar-coat the results too much.

Granted, no one wants to hear "oh no! The cards say bad, horrible things!" but no one wants the rose-colored glasses version either.

People want honesty and options. If the outcome looks grim let them know how they can change it. Think of a doctor's method. Does the doc just yell out "ahhh...you're gonna die!" or does he explain the condition, options and treatment procedures in a calm and professional manner?

Another key to reading the cards is to do it in story form. As I have tried to iterate in this book on several occasions is that you should never just read straight from a guide book for interpretations. Anyone can do this, and if this is all you do then what is the querant coming to you (or paying you) for?

They can buy their own deck and read their own book. It is okay to look at a book for a reminder, but then put it in your own words and use your own feelings, interpretation or intuition to apply it to the person and their reading.

Pick Five Things

Pick five things you want to incorporate into a performance such as "recite a blessing prior to shuffling, go over Code of Ethics with customer, have low lighting, play music, explain what Tarot is."

Pick Three Tools

Tools can enhance the ambience and incense or stones can increase one's abilities by the energy or aromas they imbue.

Having extra tools will not make a person be an expert reader, or help you to read the cards; they just open up channels for reading and create a greater level of confidence.

Decide what three tools will be essential in your readings such as Tarot cloth, gemstones, and candles. If you are unsure of what types of tools people use, check the index at the back of this book.

Shuffling and Cutting

This might seem insignificant but there are people who have certain ways they like to shuffle or have the deck cut. Another option is whether the reader will only handle the cards or will have the querant shuffle, cut or both.

Some shuffle methods involve scattering the cards all over a table and then picking them up (this also adds reversals so don't do it if you don't intend on using them), there is also shuffling like a poker deck of cards—which can be difficult with large decks—and then there is just holding the deck in your hand, cutting it, and shuffling the cards back into the deck.

Some readers cut a deck once, and some cut it three times. There are no rights or wrongs, just preferred methods.

Experiment with a few different ideas and choose which one works best for you. I tend to shuffle nine times, then cut the deck once (in reading for others I have them cut the deck).

Informing the Querant

In some instances it may be crucial to inform a querant that "this reading is for entertainment purposes only" as a disclaimer to keep yourself out of legal trouble. There may also be other things you want to talk to the querant about such as what they can expect from the reading, what you want do, your Code of Ethics (more to come on this later), their Bill of Rights, fees and time limits, etc.

Ending a Reading

How do you want to end a reading? By letting customer ask questions, by reciting a blessing, are you going to just wrap the cards up and dismiss the customer?

Ending a reading is part of the performance and can be as important as setting up the reading. For yourself you may want to jot down the layout, the cards that were laid out, and what your interpretation and feelings about the reading are.

Write Your Performance

Write your performance down like a script or directions so that you can follow it each and every time. I have created a simple checklist for myself with items such as: set the mood, read the code of ethics, help querant formulate the question, choose the appropriate layout, look for patterns, read the cards.

Your own performance is just that, your own.

Write down as much or as little as you need in a sort of checklist so that you can use the same performance each time.

A checklist for a performance might be "lay down Tarot cloth, set up and light candles, lay gemstones down in the four corners, inform the querant of the Code of Ethics, shuffle nine times, let the querant cut the deck, perform the reading.

Perform a Trial Run

Now that you have written a performance do a trial run either on yourself or on friends to see how it performs. Make whatever necessary changes are needed to create the desired atmosphere.

Readings—Rewrite into "story form"

After having done several practice readings perform a few more and put the interpretation into story form. This does not mean to write it down, but speak it out loud whether to yourself or for someone else in story-type language.

If you simply read from the book or state "this card means A-B-C" and don't try to embellish or put it into your own words, then what is the Querant coming to you for? He or she can buy their own book and do the same thing.

Stories can be a short sentence, a paragraph, or as long as you need to get the point across. An example is "in the past, I had to change my point of view in order to balance my work and social life and in the future I will see the change that I want."

This flows easier and gives the Querant a sense that you do know what you are doing when it comes to reading Tarot cards.

Get Critiqued

Perform a reading for a friend or family and have them give you a critique, write/discuss what they said they liked or didn't like. You can also use this to perfect your performance so that when you are reading for someone they feel comfortable, and you feel confident and comfortable.

Critique a Reading You Did

Critique a reading that you did for someone else—do you feel that they benefited from the reading or understood it, what positive feedback did they give you, what would you have done differently?

Receive a Reading

Nothing beats learning how to develop your own performance than by getting a reading from someone else.

Through this you can learn what you like or don't like about how the reading was conducted and what you may what to emulate (professionalism, comfort, concern) and don't want to emulate (sloppiness, too little information, too ambiguous).

Often there are businesses in towns that do readings, otherwise look for New Age, Pagan, and Renaissance festivals in the area.

If there is absolutely no local place to receive a reading consider getting one online, although many dynamics are lost through this method.

Critique the Reading

Critique the reading you received from someone else and explain/discuss what they did that you liked or didn't like. How comfortable were you with the reading and how well did the reading depicted you or your situation.

Was it helpful or not?

When receiving a reading critique like you would any other business or service and consider the following: what did you like/dislike about the reading? What would you have done different if you were the one performing the reading?

CODE OF ETHICS

A Code of Ethics if written in many different businesses and organizations and is basically is a set of by-laws or information that will protect the practitioners and the customers from legal issues or to protect members of a club or organization and ensure the fair and equal treatment of everyone involved.

If reading for yourself or friends at social gatherings you won't need a Code of Ethics, but if reading for strangers or as a business then it is advisable to have one.

There are several different codes to be found on the internet but a basic one should include something that will protect you from legal, medical, psychological or financial responsibility.

You may also want a statement declaring there is no guarantee on results so customers cannot come back and try to sue you for damages incurred based on decisions they made from a Tarot reading.

If you think this is not possible remember a woman sued and won a major fast food corporation because her coffee was hot and people have sued cigarette companies for health complications they received because of smoking.

A Code of Ethics also can state what Tarot is not such as: results are not set in stone, it does not predict a 100% certain future, it will not give you lottery numbers, and so on. You may even want to include some of the myths seen earlier such as it is not evil and will not open portals.

Whatever you include is up to you but the idea is to make the customer aware of what the session will entail and help them feel comfortable. It can be typed out and customers made to sign it, or it can be posted on a wall, kept in paperwork, or something that is handed out to customers. At the very least I recommend the following statement:

"All readings are for your enjoyment, enlightenment and entertainment. I hold no legal, medical, psychological, or financial responsibility for decisions made based on your reading. I will not read for people not in attendance or without their permission.

"Tarot is neither a substitution for seeking advice from experts in other fields nor a substitute for common sense. I offer no refunds or guarantees on outcomes of readings. I do not cast spells or rid people of demons. I will not add in extra fees that were not previously discussed prior to the reading.

"I will also not divulge the results of your readings to others; your information is kept confidential and private. However, in the event that you confess a crime I am under no obligation by HIPPA laws to keep this confidential and I can and will report you for heinous offenses or at my discretion.

This reading is for entertainment purposes only and in no way predicts a future set in stone or causes events to happen."

This will keep you in the free-and-clear from any damages or legal responsibility and in some instances, for those owning a business as a Tarot reader some form of a disclaimer may be essential in order to comply with the terms of your with the business.

A Client Bill of Rights might be a spate document or it might be included in the Code of Ethics but it is basically letting the client know, obviously, what their rights are such as privacy, confidentiality, a useful and supportive Tarot reading, and no extra or hidden fees, etc.

The website "Tarot Certification Board of America" has a Client Bill of Rights posted on their website (see bibliography for address).

Importance

Why do you think having a Code of Ethics is important when reading for others? Is this something that you are going to consider doing?

It may be essential in a business aspect due to liabilities and such, but just in personal or social situations it may not be necessary.

Research Other Codes

Check out other Code of Ethics on the internet by doing a "Google" search. Read through the codes and take note of ideas that appeal or don't appeal to you.

Use these also as inspiration to and research to writing your own. The American Tarot Association and Tarot World Network are good places to look for Codes of Ethics.

Top Five On Your List

Think about what is most important for you to convey in a reading. Then choose the top five things you will absolutely have on your Code of Ethics?

Why did you choose these five things?

Eventually you will have more than five things, but this is to get your started.

Not on the List

There may be some things you don't want or need on your Code of Ethics. Of the codes you have seen what will you not put on your list? Write or discuss why these will not be on our list.

Write a Code

Write a code of ethics that informs the querant as well as providing protection to the reader and to the querant. Keep this somewhere it can be accessed quickly.

Include at least ten things that are important for you to convey to the querants. If you are in a group, write a group Code of Ethics.

Try the Code out on Querants

This activity could be added to the practice performance or you can simply read over it with friends to give you practice on reciting it or to see what their opinions are of it. Does it make sense? Do they feel comfortable hearing it or signing off on it (if desired by the reader)? What changes need to be made, if any?

THEORIES OF TAROT

There tends to be three main theories on how or why Tarot works and while it not an exact science and no one is 100% sure how the cards work, the three most common theories tend to be one of the following or even a combination of all three:

1) Divine Intervention or Spiritual Influence;

2) Collective Unconsciousness and;

3) Personal Subconscious (a.k.a., intuition).

There might be other theories but these tend to be the basic ideas of how and why Tarot works that I have come across.

Spiritual influence or divine intervention is a common idea in various divination methods such as with spirit boards and pendulums and simply means that universe, divine entities, spirits from the other world, or the "power that be" are guiding the reading and aiding the reader in interpreting the cards.

The next two methods go hand-in-hand in psychological studies. Carl Jung (1875-1961), a noted psychiatrist and psychotherapist, theorized that there is both a personal subconscious and a collective unconscious. The personal subconscious is a personal reservoir of experiences unique to each person. This is what makes us not like a certain food, shudder if we hear a certain song, or look at abstract art and see butterflies.

The collective unconscious is a concept that "collects and organizes" those personal experiences into the experiences of a species or a region.

For example, as a result of our conditioning Americans are 'grossed-out' over eating bugs or snails because it is not part of our culture. Other regions might consider a cheeseburger gross.

This belief also is used to explain how birds know when and where to migrate or how baby sea turtles know to head for the ocean, it is an inborn knowledge passed down from the generations before.

That being said, in Tarot, the belief of a personal consciousness means that they cards work because each we interpret the images, symbols, and signs from out own personal viewpoints or meanings we attribute to what we are seeing.

We are tapping into our personal consciousness in order to attribute meaning to a card.

With the collective unconsciousness we are interpreting the cards based on a universal meaning such as it is universally accepted that foxes are attributed with cunningness so a card with a fox indicates clever, cunning, or tricky behaviors or situations.

When we read the cards we are 'tapping into' this collective unconsciousness to attribute meanings to what we see. This is also why throughout this book I challenge readers to use both the universal message of the cards and their own personal meanings.

But, regardless of the theories that are out there, Tarot works and I one doesn't necessarily need to know how or why, they only need to trust that it works.

For example, I don't need to know how the copy machine works or how a carburetor helps my car run. However, with Tarot we do not have it down to an exact science (yet) as to how it works as we do with cars and copy machines.

Tarot is a mystic and occult practice and the best explanation I have seen (I cannot remember where) is:

"Tarot works because it resonates with the soul."

Theories—Personal Subconscious or Intuition

One of the theories on how Tarot works is that it is all based on our personal interpretations, intuition, or personal sub-consciousness.

We are drawing on our personal reservoir of experiences to help us find meaning in the cards and apply this to the situation, the person, and the imagery.

Our subconscious mind is unlocked to give us the answers we already have; we are using our intuition.

This is the same as when people say we already know all of the answers, we just have to find them. How do you feel about this theory?

Theories—Collective Unconsciousness

A second theory is that the answers are all part of a collective unconsciousness and we are tapping into this to retrieve the answers.

Carl Jung coined this phrase to describe an "unconscious mind" that is expressed in humanity and all life forms that have a central nervous system.

By using the cards we are, in a sense, using keys to open the door to this collective unconscious to retrieve answers. How do you feel about this theory?

Theories—Divine or Spiritual Intervention

Another theory is that through the help of spirits, gods, or the divine we are able to interpret the images and esoteric symbolism and apply it to the Querant in a relevant manner. How do you feel about this theory?

Theories—Personal Idea

If you agree with one of the above theories explain why or if combining the theories into one, write or discuss how they work together.

You might even have a different idea then the ones listed here. If so, what is your personal theory on how and why Tarot works?

Theories—Other

Other then the three main theories, have you heard of other ideas or beliefs behind how or why Tarot works? How do you feel about these theories?

Or, what would you say to those who do not believe that Tarot works and how would you explain to them how it is possible that Tarot can reveal answers to us.

PERSONAL REFLECTIONS

In the earlier part of this book I mentioned how there were times I wanted to do something—*anything*—with and the next two sections are a direct result of that need. Instead of always doing readings I wanted to see what the cards would say about certain situations.

Choosing Tarot cards, whether on purpose or randomly, to represent certain situations or as answers to 'life's questions' is not only interesting but it provides a greater connection to the cards, adds your energy to them, helps to develop insight into their meanings, and helps you to interpret the messages within.

A person can sit and watch television, think of a topic, and just pull a card to see what comes up.

The idea to use Tarot cards this way came about simply as I went about my daily life. Often a situation would occur and I would immediately think "this is (blank) card moment!"

For example, at work ridiculous daily task was implemented that a co-worker and I had to execute. I remember thinking "this is a foolish endeavor" and that made me think of The Fool card.

This helped me to keep the situation in perspective meaning that if I remained carefree and light-hearted, that is to not stress over it, others would see how ridiculous it was. Sure enough, the 'higher-ups' realized what it was costing us and that it was impractical.

There have been other times, too, when a person or a situation has made me think of a Tarot card and I gain inspiration or advice on how to deal with them or it based on what I know about that card.

For those who use Tarot on a regular basis, study it in-depth, or find a real connection with it will perhaps start to see Tarot meanings in everything we do or experience.

Interests—Choosing a Card

Pick three-five cards that fit with your interests, desires, sports, personality, traits, or hobbies and write/discuss why those cards fit.

For example, three of cups could indicate being in a dance class or seven of pentacles a gardening club.

Interests—Applications

After doing the previous activity, pull a card at random and see if that applies to your hobby, etc. Be objective, you might not realize it does until you see the card.

For example, if you have a card depicting volunteer time/charity work and then pull the devil card you may come to realize that the charity work is a self-imposed bond that you feel you are doing because you have to and you no longer enjoy it but don't think you can stop.

What Would Tarot Do

Pick a past or current situation in your life where Tarot either did help or could have helped you overcome it. What advice or information is Tarot giving you about that situation?

Tarot and Your Family

Think of your extended or immediate family and sort through the deck choosing a card that best represents each family member. Then sit and place all the cards on a flat surface and choose other cards to represent the relationships.

For example, your parents might individually be represented by the High Priestess and Magician but together they are represented by the Lovers.

Or you and an older sibling are represented as Strength and the Empress but the relationship between you two is seen as the Six of Cups.

Maybe it is the Eight of Cups if a sibling has turned their back on you and no longer has contact with you.

Current Events and Tarot

Look at current or past social situations, major media coverage, scandals, news, or historical events and pick a Tarot card that fits with that situation.

For example, the Tower card might represent the sinking of the

Titanic in that it was a major upheaval. Or perhaps the Ten of Swords is a political scandal (being stabbed in the back). Write key words for the event and the card and see how they compare, or even pull one card to see what lesson should have been learned from that event or what changes were made (such as with Titanic cruise ship regulations, particularly concerning the number of lifeboats, changed).

Problem Solving

Think of a problem you have and deliberately choose a card that fits that situation. Then, shuffle or cut the remaining deck and draw a card at random to show how you can go about resolving the problem.

Becoming the Person You Want to Be

Pick a card that represents who or where you are today.

Then, pick a card depicting who you want to be in the future. For example; if you are a Page (which can sometimes depict a student) and you want to obtain a degree then your future self might be the High Priestess.

Now, shuffle the remaining deck and randomly draw one to three cards to show how you can get there.

In the example given these three cards might show qualities such as studying, concentration, and focus.

Ridding Self of Bad Habits

In a reverse aspect, you can use Tarot to figure out how to get rid of bad habits you have.

Choose one to three cards representing the negative aspects of yourself or things you want to change (you may want or need to use reversals for this).

Then, shuffle the remaining deck and randomly draw one to three cards to show how you can go about eliminating or changing these habits.

Birth Year

Using just your birth year, lay cards out in corresponding numbers from the Majors and see if or how they can tie into some aspect of your life (present, past or future).

For example, my birth year is 1972 so I would have the Magician (1) the Hermit (9), The Chariot (7) and the High Priestess (2).

They tie into my life in that I am a seeker of knowledge (hermit); my spiritual beliefs (magician and high priestess); and my career as an author (Chariot).

Represent You the Most

Sort through the deck and choose three cards that represent you the most? Write or discuss why you chose these cards and how they represent you.

Represent You the Least

Sort through the deck and choose three cards that represent you the least. Write or discuss why you chose these cards and how they represent you.

Good vs. Evil

Pick your "ultimate good" and "ultimate bad" card—that is, what card fits your good side of you and what card represents the inner-dark or bad side of your personality?

Past, Present Future—Chosen

Flip through the deck and choose one card each to represent your past, present, or future self (where or who you want to be years from now). Write/discuss why you chose these cards and how they represent you.

Past, Present Future—Random

Shuffle the cards and randomly draw three to represent your past, present and future self. Do you agree or disagree with the cards drawn? How do they compare with the cards you chose in the above activity?

Children

If you have children, draw one card at random for each child. Spend some time writing key words or an interpretation, or look back at the ones you have already written, and see if these cards fit your children's personalities or life. If you don't have any, think about children you know such as nieces, or nephews.

You can also go back to the Querant or significator card section and choose a card for your children using one of those methods.

Relationships

If looking currently single but wanting a spouse or long-time partner, draw a card and write-discuss the personality type associated with the card. Why do you want that type of person?

Or, choose three cards that represent the current relationship you are in (or why you are single) and write/discuss why you chose those cards.

You can also choose cards that show the type of relationship you want to have and choose one extra card to show what you need to do to achieve that.

What's My Personality

Instead of (or in addition to) doing a querant card just ask Tarot "what is my personality type" and pull a card. Write or discuss what personality type it describes and whether or not you agree that this accurately describes you.

What's My Mood?

Just like a mood ring, see if Tarot can describe your current mood. Ask the question and then pull a card and see if it accurately describes the mood you are in. What in the card gave you indications that determined your mood?

Think about the general feel or mood of the card, the attitudes of the people in it, or the colors used and how all these are indicative to your mood.

My Purpose in Life

Pull one to three cards at random while considering what your purpose in life is. What does the card say, does this fit with the current path you are on or what you feel is your purpose in life?

Tarot & the Meaning of Life

As I said in the previous section, most of these were devised because of my desire to want to do something with Tarot but not necessarily a reading. I sat on the couch one day wondering and thinking to myself what Tarot would say about various topics.

For this book I tried to think of all the major topics that are often taboo or very controversial in society. But, while these are serious topics I would not take the answers seriously as the questions are ambiguous and have no right or wrong answers.

This is just a fun exercise meant to get readers used to handling their cards and interpreting the images. It makes for some neat journal entries or group discussions.

These questions are definitely a case of the personal subconscious theory at work here in that your upbringing, culture, religion, family and personal beliefs, all are playing a role in how you view what the cards are saying.

If you absolutely do not believe in the existence of aliens and draw the Judgment card then you might see this as interpreting that man should only have a belief in God or angels and the naked humans indicate we are made in his image.

For those who do believe in aliens the angel in the sky might be interpreted as a non-human being, i.e. an alien, and the naked humans show our vulnerability and naiveté in thinking we are the only sentient beings in the universe.

One to three cards can be pulled for each of these and use the key words, symbolism, numbers, colors, people, animals, patterns, and elements that you have previously learned about to guide you in determine what the card is saying about each of the following concepts. The elements can be used based on the realms they rule.

For example, if pulling a card with the water element for the question on religion it may indicate that it is an emotional need.

However, same question but a pentacle card might indicate a physical need—which would imply we need or want religion based on a physical need to be around like-minded people or for that sense of community.

Each of the topics has multiple questions (just like most of the other entries in this book) and each one can be addressed or just choose certain ones to ask the cards.

Oh, and by the way…let me remind you again that these are just for fun and as exercises. I don't want to see any articles, blogs, or other media saying it's okay to be racist but not homosexual or that one religion is better than another because "Tarot says so."

Tarot is based on individual experiences and intuition, and these exercises are only to see what interpretations you can get out of the cards, which is all based on your personal subconscious or experiences; the cards are *not* saying what is right or wrong.

Religion

Religion is a much-debated topic and one that society as a whole cannot agree on. Everyone has a different belief, even individuals within a religion.

Thinking about your own religious beliefs or religion as a whole concept pull a card or cards to determine what is religion and why man feels he needs it, or doesn't need it?

What do the cards say about different religions, spiritual beliefs, or Atheism?

Tarot

Tarot is used for many reasons and there are many theories as to how or why it works, think about the purpose of Tarot and pull a card or cards to show what the purpose of Tarot is and why some of us feel we need it or benefit from it.

Aliens

Another heated topic with beliefs being that they don't exist; they do but haven't visited; they have visited only in recent times; and even to that they are responsible for our existence.

Pull cards to reveal what Tarot has to say on the existence of aliens. If interpreted as existing, pull another card to show what they want with the human race.

Abortion

Perhaps no topic (other then same-gender marriages) has received more attention in the courts and political campaigns as this one. People tend to stick to three beliefs: Pro-Choice, Pro-Life, or maybe don't care at all.

Think about the concept and pull cards to see what Tarot has to say about abortion.

Death

I would find it very interesting to pull the Death card for this question. It would be almost ironic but also as good of an answer as you can get, either you will view it as the universal meaning such as transformation or change (from one life to another) or literally—death means death.

However, the chances of drawing this card for this question is not great so you will have to use your creative intuition to determine what other cards are saying about death, it's purpose, or how we should view it (some see it as a time of grief, others as a celebration or "going home").

Racism and Prejudice

A topic I feel very strongly about. Treat people as people and judge them based on personality not religion, disability, race or ethnicity.

Society has made many strides towards eradicating much of this but there will always be individuals or groups who are racist or prejudice towards certain things or people. Pull cards to determine why it exists, will society ever be free of it, or what people can do to eradicate racism and prejudice in their own life.

Homosexuality

Another topic heatedly debated and another in which I believe "we should treat people as people" and not worry about sexual preference.

Our upbringing, culture, and religion give each of us a very firm belief in it being right or wrong. But I wonder what Tarot says about it?

Politics

Politics is a very intricate topic and one that most of us could probably do with a little enlightenment.

Pick cards at random to show what the purpose is of politics or what our personal reward is from it.

Try determining the outcome of a political race using Querant cards to depict the two opponents and drawing one to three cards to either determine if they will win or to show their campaign platform.

Polygamist Relationships

Some cultures and religions believe it is okay to have more than one spouse whereas others consider it taboo. Pull cards to determine what the advantages or disadvantages are from a polygamist marriage (such as extra help with the children, or having to share your husband).

Mankind's Purpose

Ahh...the question that will never be answered; we, as a society and as individuals, have all wondered what our purpose is here on this planet. Perhaps not even the Tarot cards know the answer to this question, but pull a card and see what it says about our purpose on this planet.

Balance

The good, the bad; the dark and the light; work versus play; and the yin-and the yang. Balance is everywhere and some people theorize we have evil so that we will know what good is.

We need a basis for comparison; how do we know what good is without evil to compare it to? Randomly select least two cards and see if they balance or oppose each other in their ideas.

Or, ask what do we need to keep balance in the universe or in ourselves and randomly select a card for the answer.

The Earth

Mankind has a purpose—it must or else why are we here—but what is the purpose of the earth? Is it just a place we call home, just something we can use for our own purposes and then move onto the next one when we use up its resources?

Is it an experiment by aliens or gods? Is it its own entity and actually a living, breathing thing—a supernatural entity in a sense? What is the purpose or mission of Earth as a planet or life force?

Universe

Our universe exists—we know that. But theories abound that other universes exist as well, other galaxies, solar systems, dimensions, or worlds.

Pull cards to see what Tarot says about their existence and why they might exist, or what people get out of either not believing or by believing in their existence.

Gods and Deities

One god or multiple gods, this topic is very controversial with people having a firm idea that their belief is right. Ancients believed in multiple deities and each culture had its own set of names, patrons, and personalities. Many major religions belief in monotheism, or one deity.

What does Tarot say about our beliefs in gods and why mankind feels a need to believe in a supreme being.

Afterlife

Another question we do not 100% know the answers to or rely on only faith to tell us what is in the afterlife. Pull cards to see what the purpose of it is (a reward, punishment, the end of a cycle) or what happens when we die.

Hopefully no one gets the Devil card for this one because despite the card meaning self-imposed bonds, no one wants to ask "what is the afterlife" and get the stereotypical image of hellfire, brimstone and a devil (however, if you do remember the card means 'self-imposed restraints' so it may mean we will be free from restraints).

Reincarnation

In addition to the beliefs of the afterlife there are some who believe we are reincarnated and that this is so because we need to learn lessons, we only ascend to a paradise after we have learned those lessons.

There is also Karma that states what we do in this life can affect outcomes in the next life, so we better live well. Assuming reincarnation is real ask Tarot what its purpose is.

Animals

Animals are all around us and in so many species and forms it is impossible to count them all and with new species being discovered all the time.

Randomly select cards determine what purpose animals serve on the earth or in our lives?

You can also pull cards to determine the plausibility of crypto-creatures (Loch Ness Monster, Bigfoot, and et.al.) and why we like to or tend to believe in them.

Knowledge

Esoteric, practical, mundane and magical…man is always on a quest for knowledge and that is what the Hermit card typically represents.

Why is mankind always seeking knowledge instead of being content with what we currently know?

What is the purpose of man having cognizant thought and being able to rationalize, solve problems and reason?

Family & Social Groupings

Families mean something different to everyone: reverence of the elderly; extended family situations, small families; large families; and some are not even blood-ties.

Whatever our beliefs or practices, there seems to be a need for social connections.

Ask the cards why we have this need. What purpose does a community, family, or social group give us? If we did not have this, what would life be like?

TAROT SPELLS AND MEDITATION

When I first started studying Tarot I had no idea that I could use the cards in spells. As a practitioner of herbal, nature, gemstones and candle magic I was ecstatic to learn I could add in yet one more of my favorite things.

I think I had seen a spell online involving Tarot cards as the focus for intent and from there I discovered one of favorite Tarot books ever, "Tarot Spells" by Janina Renee. This book has spells for all occasions and is a must-have if interested in Tarot spells. Since buying the book I have even created my own Tarot spells or blessings.

The cards work great for intent such as showing what is wanted out of the spell (money, romance, protection, etc.) or the cards can be used to help represent the elements such as placing a pentacle suit card in the earth quarter of an altar, a cups suit card in the water quarter, and so on.

Using Tarot cards in spells is beneficial because they aid in visualization, they are portable, and they are charged with energy.

Querant or Significator cards can also be used to represent the person the spell is for (either yourself or someone else) or a card can be placed on an altar and used as a focal point for focusing energy on.

Using them in spells also helps a person to learn the cards well as you need to know which cards best represent aspects of the spell, such as the goal or intent.

The spells listed in this section are basic and simple to perform to appeal to all levels, but there is more complex or specialized spells on the internet and in books.

Again, I recommend "Tarot Spells" for anyone wanting to learn more. The ones here are just to give readers an idea of what is involved in a Tarot spell and hopefully to introduce a new and exciting way to use the cards.

Meditation is also a big topic right now with people from all walks of life and different faiths believing in its benefits and using it on a daily or weekly basis.

Meditation can be done in a variety of ways and Tarot is yet one more way to meditate. The cards become the focal point of a meditation and give the eyes and mind something to do to keep it from wandering to mundane thoughts.

I have listed four basic and simple meditative practices but there may be others or you may create your own method.

Basic Spell

For a very basic spell, think of the intent (money, friends, getting over shyness), and choose a card that represents that intent or purpose.

If you need multiple cards to show the intent properly that's fine, but don't go over three cards as it can confuse or muddle the energies.

Set the cards down on an altar or table.

Next, light a candle that represents the intent (look in the appendixes in the back of this book for colors and their symbolism).

Ask the candle is lit recite the following verse, or make up your own verse:

> *Harming none and blessed be, help this spell manifest for me.*
> *Harming none and blessed be send positive energies to me.*
> *Harming none and blessed be, I cast this spell, so mote it be.*

Visualize what you want to happen and when it is firmly in your mind, either extinguish the candle let it burn down.

If allowing it to burn down let the card(s) remain near it so the light reflects on them. If extinguishing it, visualize the smoke taking the prayer/intent up to the gods, then insert the card back into the center of the deck and shuffle once to cast the energies out to do their work.

Achieve a Goal Spell

For this spell you will need a white and black candle to represent balance and opposing forces. This can be done at an altar with the elemental correspondences being represented or in a simpler fashion at the kitchen table with just the candles and cards.

Think of a goal you want to achieve. As an example, I will use "buying a home" as a goal.

Next, think of the steps required to achieve that goal such as: contact a realtor, get approved for a loan, and find a house fitting your needs.

Then, sort through a deck and pull out cards to show the intent and each of the steps in your goal. Once you have your cards set the

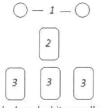

1 black and white candles
2 goal card
3 step cards

candles at the far end of the table or altar, place the black candle on the left and the white candle on the right side.

Below the candles place the intent card. Below that, place the 'step' cards in the order they need to be achieved from left to right. Light the candles, and touching each card recite the following:

This, my goal, I want to achieve, may it harm none & none shall grieve.
These are the steps, I must meet each one before my purpose will be done.
With every card shown I will reap the benefits of what I have sown.

Take a few minutes to close your eyes and visualize yourself completing each step and finally achieving the goal. When the vision is firm in your mind and you feel confident in making the goal a reality, open your eyes.

Either extinguish the candles with a candle snuffer or let them burn down (leaving the cards next to them until they do). Then put everything away.

A Positive Change Spell

This spell is for the purpose of making positive changes in your self. Choose a card that most represents you and a card that represents where you want to be in life or what changes you want to make.

For example, perhaps you have an addiction so you choose the Devil card (self-imposed restraints).

But, you want to break the addiction and perhaps help others through the same process so you choose the High Priestess to represent this.

Or, it might be a situation such as going from student (a Page card) to a teacher or leader (King, Queen, Hierophant or High Priestess).

On a table or an altar set the card down representing who you are now on the left side. Above this card, place a black candle.

On the right side of the space place the card representing who you want to be or where you want to go in life and above this card place a white candle.

Recite the following verse:

From this to that, and here to there
I ask to grow, to change and as each step is met
or obstacle is overcome I know I will become the person

I envision for my self and who I was meant to be.

Carefully slide first the black candle towards the center, and then the card representing who you are now.

Then, slide the white candle and its card towards the center but leaving a space between the two sides still as you will slide these each day for seven days until they meet "in the middle."

Extinguish the candles and leave them and the cards set up. The next day, around the same time if possible, perform this again by lighting first the black candle, and then the white, recite the verse, and slide the candles towards each other.

On the seventh day after you have performed the above steps finish off the spell by reciting:

From past to present I now can see
I am truly becoming who I am meant to be.

Leave everything, letting the candles burn for an extra hour, and then put everything away. Put the cards back into the center of the deck and shuffle once to spread the energies.

Write a Tarot Spell of Your Choice

Writing Tarot spells is almost as addicting as writing spreads. It can be simple or complex, focused on a certain topic, or a general spell. It can involve several cards or just one.

I have done spells in which I pick three cards to represent a need or area in my life then write a spell around it.

If unfamiliar with Paganism and spell-writing take some time to research it in books or on the internet to get the method and formula down.

Or, if not interested in spells just use this task as a prayer task by simply setting a card or cards on a flat surface and light some candles, sort of like a prayer vigil or shrine but using cards as the focal point.

Writing a spell using Tarot cards is similar to writing a Tarot Spread.

You will need: intent or purpose, tools, and a Tarot deck. From there, what you add or how it is performed is simply up to you.

Tarot Meditation #1

A good method for mediation is to pick a specific card, either one you like or one that has meaning for you and coincides with a situation you are going through.

Sit in a quiet and comfortable place and look at the card, memorizing every detail and nuance of it.

Then, close your eyes but hold onto that image picturing it as a card first, then growing larger and the borders of the card falling away and the images becoming three-dimensional, until all you see is just the scenery or people as if it is real.

When that image is strong and firm in your mind, picture yourself stepping into the scene.

Walk around, visualize things from a different angle, talk to people and have them respond to you, pretend you are in a real scenario and interacting with it.

When you feel you have gained whatever knowledge you can, come back to the entrance of the scene and step out, imagining the scene getting smaller and smaller until it is just a card again.

Write down what you experienced.

Tarot Meditation #2

On a flat surface such as a table or altar, pick out a card that has meaning to you or use your power card and set it up so that it stands up (a plate stand or business card holder works great for this).

Place a candle on either side of the card so that light reflects onto it and turn the lights in the room low.

Listen to some soothing music, burn some incense, or whatever you need to do to set the mood.

Stare at the card using it as a focal point, start off noticing details of the card but eventually your mind will wander, let it and see where it takes you.

You might come to terms with or learn something knew about yourself by relaxing and just letting your mind go.

You can also do this as a writing exercise by describing the card to start off with and then writing whatever comes to your mind.

Tarot Meditation #3

Go back to the section on Querant, Power and Signifactor cards and figure yours out by one of the methods mentioned (if you haven't already).

Pull that card from the deck and meditate actively on it by writing what you see, literally, in the card (describe the scene, the people, etc), then write all the key words you can think of, write a key phrase, and write a basic interpretation for the card.

Now look at all you have written, does it apply to you? Are there traits the card has that you don't have yet but want (such as leadership skills).

Reflect on how you can become more like the card and perhaps even create goals for yourself to acquire those skills or knowledge.

Tarot Meditation #4

Choose nine cards that represent your desires, wishes or goals (do not randomly select but actually look through the cards and make conscious choices).

Divide those three cards down to groups of threes, organizing them in whatever way fits.

For example, if you chose the 5 of Wands, 5 Cups, 5 Swords, Hanged Man, High Priestess, Moon, 3 Pentacles, 2 Pentacles, Queen Pentacles then group the ones numbered five, the three majors, and the three Pentacle cards.

Some groupings may not be as obvious as this and you may have to look at the meaning of the cards or symbols in the card.

Then, for each group, lay the cards in order of importance (so you will have a grid pattern, the three "five" cards in one row, the three majors in another, and the three pentacles in a row).

Now, touch each card and state its purpose such as "this is a card of change' and reflect on what that means or how that applies to the situation you are meditating on. Do this for all nine cards.

Record your observations.

Daily Meditation

On whatever day this activity is done, add up the full date and if it is a number higher than 21 reduce it to a single digit.

Then look at the Major Arcana that shares that number and divine what the day means or will bring based on the card's typical meaning. For example, if today is 07/05/2012 the reduced number is 17.

In the Major Arcana this is The Star which may mean that everything will go right today, that all wishes will come true or a person should reach for the stars as they just might get what they are wishing for.

This can also be done using the Minor Arcana and using seasonal correspondences to determine which of the suits to use; for numbers higher than 10 reduce it to a single digit.

For example, if the date were 04/06/2012 the number of all the numbers added up is 15. Add the one and the five to get six.

Since the month is April, which is spring, use the suit of wands so pull the Six of Wands to see what today's meaning is.

Write A Meditation

Following the examples above, write a method of meditation.

Make sure to include any additional tools needed (music, candles, etc), how many cards to use, the method for choosing cards (conscious choice or random), approximately how much time to spend on the meditation, what to do with the results, and anything else you can think of that is pertinent.

ARTS & CRAFTS

It might seem weird to have a section on arts and crafts in a Tarot book, but for those who are crafty and like Tarot the two items go hand-in-hand. There are a number of Tarot accessories that can be made such as Tarot cloths, pouches, boxes or carrying cases, and decorating a Tarot journal.

Many Tarot enthusiasts like to customize and create accessories for their cards but there are also things that craft or artsy people can do that makes them feel connected with Tarot such as creating jewelry inspired by Tarot, creating a set of "Tarot Runes" or tiles (see entry titled Tarot Tiles) or even scrapbooking events where they have done Tarot readings.

I have a locket I purchased at an arts and crafts store that I placed an entire deck of miniature cards inside (the cards are just pictures of Rider Waite cards shrunken in a word program to about ½ inch big and 'laminated' with tape). When I wear it I feel that I have the power and wisdom of Tarot with me wherever I go.

Coloring or making a deck is also considered "arts and crafts" even if it is created on the computer with digital images. There are sets of cards that are sold called "color your own" decks and there are several sites where cards can be printed and colored in by hand.

There are also several mediums in which a person can create their own deck such as painting, colored pencils, digital images, or photography.

None of the following prompts are essential for learning Tarot but they are fun and neat ideas to do if a person wants to feel connected with Tarot but not necessarily study or do readings.

There are websites devoted to arts and crafts regarding Tarot such as "Tarot Inspired Craft Projects" at About.Com (see Bibliography for URL).

Create a Journal

Tarot journals are a lot of fun and can be simple projects outlinging you're your disclaimer or Code of Ethics, a few key notes on the card's universal interpretations or the performance set-up.

They can also be complex and contain answers to the prompts or exercises in this book, your own interpretations of the cards, records of every reading you have done, etc. They can be made in computer programs, in a tablet, a bound journal, or three-ring binders.

Three-ring binders and computers are good for the extra-organized who like to have things separated or in sections but journals are great for those who like a more homespun feel.

Some topics to consider when creating a journal might be:

1) Spreads & Layouts

2) Record of Readings

3) Card Interpretations

4) Key Phrases

5) Key Words

6) Code of Ethics

7) Card Blessings

8) Reading Performance

9) Wish List of Decks

10) Deck Reviews

11) Spells & Meditation

12) Journal or Creative Writing Prompts

13) Color, Number, Elemental and Symbol Meanings.

Of course, each person may have their own ideas of categories to add or might jut record experiences, readings and such as they occur in a chronological order.

The key to remember in creating a journal is use what works for you, personalize it, and be creative!

Tarot Jewelry

I had printed out some small pictures of Tarot cards, laminated them (with tape) and then inserted them into clear glass locket that I found at a craft store.

You can also decoupage them onto flat pendants to create earrings or necklaces. I have even seen paper beads made from Tarot images printed from the computer.

There are also Italian Charm bracelets which are small square or rectangle charms that fit together and they have a wide variety of designs or styles. Search EBay or other sites for charms made with Tarot images and create your own unique bracelet.

Tarot Tiles

Another craft I did was to purchase square tiles (like Scrabble ™ tiles) from a craft store and I glued on printed images of the Rider Waite decks.

The tiles are a little less than one-inch square but enough to see what the card is, although some of the symbols and such are lost being so small.

I then sprayed them with clear varnish and let them dry.

I placed them in a pouch and now I have Tarot tiles, which I will sometimes ask a simple question, shake the bag, and then pull out a tile and interpret its meaning.

Tarot I-Ching

I-Ching is a set of yarrow sticks that are tossed down and messages are interpreted in the patterns of the sticks.

Create your own I-Ching sticks by writing a card name on a popsicle stick.

Place the sticks in a bag and pull out how many you need for the spread, just like you would if you were dealing Tarot cards.

Or, you can reach into a bag or box and grab a small handful, drop the sticks down and read them based on the patterns they make. For example, the the Three of Swords lays over a King card what might this mean?

If you wrote the names on only side of the stick then use the blank side as a reversal (although you will have to turn it over to see what it is).

This method is a real challenge in that you have no images with which to interpret the cards by.

Tarot Rosary

This is on my "to-do" list but if anyone reading this creates one, please let me know and I will consider trading a book, Tarot cards, or buying it from them.

As a child I loved the concept of Rosary beads, my mother had them and she took such comfort from them. But, not being raised Catholic I never knew how to use them and now that I am Pagan the Catholic Rosary will not suffice. But a Pagan or Tarot set would be amazing.

The Major Arcana would work best for this, otherwise it would have to be seventy-eight beads and that is a lot to remember.

If you can find or make beads already depicting the Major Arcana use those, otherwise find shaped beads or charms that might fit the Major Arcana.

String them together and when needing comfort, pass each bead through your fingers reciting a key phrase of that Major.

For example "as the fool I am naïve and optimistic, as the

magician I know I have the right tools, as the High Priestess I know when to pass along secrets and when to keep them" and so on. This can lend comfort or be a guide in stressful situations.

Decorate a Tarot or Keepsake Box

Decorate a wooden or cardboard box purchased from a crafts store to keep Tarot cards or Tarot related items in. Extra cards in a deck or cards from incomplete decks can be glued onto boxes and covered with a clear coat of shellac or varnish.

Or, cut out pictures from magazines that have a "Tarot" feel to them and glue onto boxes. Boxes can also be hand painted, wood burned, or stenciled.

I have also seen a tray, like a breakfast-in-bed type of tray, which was decorated with Tarot cards and then used as a coffee table centerpiece with a candle set on it.

Make a Tarot Cloth, Pouches or Wraps

A Tarot cloth can be easily "made" simply by buying a decorative handkerchief or bandana. Material can also be purchased but then the sides need to be hemmed to keep it from fraying.

The idea is to place the cards in the pocket and wrap the remaining fabric around them. This acts as a barrier between random energies in the air and the cards. It can then be lain down on the table and the cards set on them when reading—also as a barrier from mundane or random energies.

Anoint the cloth with a drop or two of essential oil, let it dry, and then wrap the cards in it for extra blessing or consecrating.

Pouches can also be sewn to keep the cards in: buy material, measure it against the cards so they will fit in it, hem all sides with a ¼ inch seam, then sew three sides together.

On the open side tie it after the cards are placed inside or create a drawstring fastener.

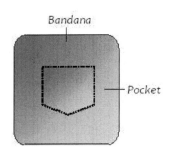

Embellishments can be added for even more decorative flair. I met a woman once who made Tarot cloths that had pockets in the center, the idea was to place the cards in the pocket then wrap the cloth around. When it was laid flat it could also act as a Tarot cloth for laying the cards on.

Collages, Framed Art, Décor

In a discussion board I was in, the question of what to do with decks that the reader no longer uses but doesn't want to trade in, or for decks that are missing cards was discussed.

The poster was asking what can those decks be used for as a means of repurposing them. Some suggestions were as bookmarkers, use in collage to decorate keepsake boxes or end tables, as scrapbook embellishments, or make collages for framed art.

Make Flash Cards

To quiz yourself or others on Tarot you can create a set of flash cards. On index cards write key phrases, description, interpretation, key words, or numerical + elemental significance (e.g., balancing finances) on one side of the card. On the other side write what the card is (two of pentacles). Hold the cards up and quiz yourself or each other.

Trimming Decks

I include this only because it is something people discuss in message boards.

A lot of Tarot collectors, it seems, do not like borders on their cards as it detracts from the pictures, which has led to the popular trend of trimming the borders.

The only concerns to consider are that the deck may be less easily sold or traded by trimming, it decreases any collector's value (some decks are quite valuable) and if the person doesn't trim carefully it can diminish the aesthetic quality of the deck.

Tarot Scrapbook

Creating a Tarot Scrapbook can be a very rewarding project for those who like to scrapbook.

If you do readings at fairs and such, have someone take a picture of you at each fair or festival you have done, or use the scrapbook to record readings you have done for yourself using embellishments that depict the reading's purpose or outcome (there is no end to the themes of embellishments a person can buy).

In my scrapbook I include pictures of the Tarot cards I have seen in unusual stores (I bought a deck at Dollar Tree and one at Michael's Arts & Crafts). I also have a magazine clipping of a feminine product ad that was done like a Tarot card.

Try incorporating journal ideas into it as well by creating pages for the cards using an image (printed off the computer) and writing your own interpretations of the card, use your scrapbook just for Tarot spells, take pictures of layouts you like or have created and insert these into the scrapbook.

The ideas are endless and it can be a very neat project to share with others. For groups, create a group Tarot book with pictures of the members and their Tarot card counterpart, pictures of Tarot events or entries for group readings.

CREATE A DECK, CARD OR THEME

I don't know of any Tarot reader who has not, at some point, attempted (and possibly succeeded) at creating their own Tarot deck. At the very least they have said "I wish there was a deck on—."

Creating your own deck or theme is very engaging, a long-term goal, very rewarding and gives a much deeper understanding of Tarot cards and their universal meaning then virtually any other form of studying the cards.

In order to be able to create the equivalent of a card I need to know a lot about the card and to have an understanding if it.

Even creating Oracle decks still helps enthusiasts create a broader sense of themselves, their world, and everything around them, and is often easier because one does not have to stick to the seventy-eight cards, four suits and Major Arcana format.

Those with artistic talents can draw their own images or non-artists can either collaborate with an artist or use images from clip art, the internet, or photographs we have taken.

The themes are also endless from basic concepts, deities, elemental correspondences, mythologies or religions, popular media, historical events, cultures, current events, sports, hobbies, careers, and just about anything else a person can come up with.

However, keep in mind that if you are using images that you have not taken or drawn yourself it is *copyright infringement* and this is very serious!

Additionally, if you use a theme from popular media such as the Twilight, Harry Potter, Charmed, Buffy or other books or TV shows this is also *copyright infringement* even if you use your own images. You did not come up with that concept on your own.

Permission can often be granted by the creators to use either their images or your own images but if you don't have that, you can't publish your deck or sell it in any fashion.

For books that no longer hold a copyright such as the Fairy Tales or works of Shakespeare, you can use these themes. If ever in doubt, contact the copyright office at www.copyright.gov.

That being said, certain themes are up for grabs as long as you use your own imagery such as supernatural creatures, objects, vampires, zombies, deities, herbs, and other such broad concepts.

Creating themes, cards, and decks is an excellent way to pass the time and for groups they can create a group deck that is unique to the group's purpose and its members. Be creative, and have fun!

Color Your Own Deck

My first deck was a Rider-Waite set that was in black and white line drawings downloaded from the internet and printed onto cardstock paper. My daughters and I colored pictures and then I placed the cardstock in a cold tea bath to stain them. I let them dry and then cut out the individual cards. I now have a set of cards that looks like a very old deck.

Of course, not everyone has to do this; there are color-your-won decks sold on the market. Cards can also be laminated to protect them. Spending time making or coloring a deck really adds some personal energy to the cards that comes out in the readings. Remember, when coloring the cards you can use your own color correspondences.

Create A Theme

Come up with your own theme for a deck, it can be a theme already out there but how would you stylize it differently?

For those not wanting to create an entire deck, just describe what theme you would like to see in a deck and why?

In a few words describe some cards you'd have in your theme and write key words, phrases or descriptions for the meanings of the cards. Describe any similarities or differences to already published decks.

As a group exercise pick a theme and decide if it would be an Oracle deck or Tarot deck and discuss what images and concepts would be included.

Create A Card

Prior to creating an entire you can start with just one card. Choose an image from a magazine, internet, or a photo and after studying it for some time jot down key words, phrases, and brief interpretation.

It can be an Oracle-style card in that it does not belong to a suit, or you can draw or look for images that correspond to a card in a Tarot deck.

For example, maybe you see a picture in a magazine of a dog with a stick in his mouth and decide to make this the Ace of Wands. Glue pictures onto cardboard or cardstock and laminate it.

This is a good group exercise as well and everyone can create their own card, then trade cards and see what others come up with for interpretations and whether it coincides with your own.

Think of other mediums to use as well such as painting, wood burning, foam or felt pieces, or even several pictures as a collage to make the card.

Create A Deck

Making a deck is time-consuming but very rewarding.

Draw, paint, cut out pictures from magazines or use clipart. Decks do not have to be the standard seventy-eight cards as seen in Rider Waite but should be of at least twenty cards to make them usable.

Keep in mind using someone else's images is not allowed without permission, but if you are making a deck for personal use and not for profit then there is no end to what you can do!

Give Them Flair!

You know that Tarot has a lot of symbolism in it. How are you going to incorporate the elements, animals, symbols, or numbers into your deck and what correspondences will they have? What key words or phrases would you add for your deck?

Non-Tarot Images

Take pictures from a camera or look for pictures online or in magazines and pretend it is a Tarot card.

Write an interpretation for it. This is good for group projects as well, with each person writing a Tarot interpretation for a specific image and comparing the differences or similarities.

Posting a picture in a message board and asking members to treat it as a Tarot card and write interpretations for it also sparks some interesting comments.

This is a good starting project for eventually creating your own deck.

Create a Deck on Popular Media

If you haven't already, create a deck (or even just the Major Arcana) based on popular media. You can use actual images from the internet or just write or discuss what cards would be created.

For example, with a Harry Potter theme who would be the High Priest and Priestess? What role would Harry Potter have?

Can the popular TV show "The Walking Dead" be used for Tarot? What role does Rick or Daryl play? What about the zombies? Can a whole new suit be created just for zombies with other suits being broken down into fighters, healers, and farmers?

Have fun with this and don't take it too seriously, it is just an exercise of the mind and meant to be used as a creative and fun outlet.

Coupon Tarot

In Patricia Telesco's "Kitchen Witch Guide to Divination" she suggests using coupons as Tarot cards. I think this is a very neat idea, and again it stretches the imagination and broadens a person's perspective on the cards and confidence in reading them.

After all, if you can get meaning out of a coupon for Gain® laundry detergent then you certainly can read a card with much more symbolism and imagery!

Flip through magazines or the Sunday paper and clip coupons that appeal to you, get some from all different areas such as food, drink, personal needs, soaps, or house wares.

Sift through them reading the ad or coupon, looking for key words such as "new and improved" and thinking about what the product is for (food is sustenance, soap is cleansing such as washing away the old, tables are stability). S

Some examples might be: Joy ™ dish soap indicating all is well and good things are coming, whereas one for diapers might mean that the querant needs to protect themselves from mishaps or accidents.

Clue the images onto index cards and laminate for a permanent set or as a group just have fun going through ads and coupons and giving interpretations on how you feel it could be used.

You can also do this just as a journal entry on five different coupons or ads if you don't want to actually make a complete deck or card.

Symbols only Deck

As an extra challenge write, discuss or actually create a symbols-only deck of about twenty symbols. Such things as hearts, dollar signs, infinity symbols, geometric shapes, signs, stars, the moon and sun, and many more symbols can all be used.

If simply writing or discussing what you'd use don't forget key words and phrases.

If actually creating a deck make them as simplistic or as complex as you want, and think about what other images would be in the card to enhance the meaning.

CREATIVE WRITING PROMPTS

When I first started practicing Tarot I had never thought to use it for writing (other than writing a book *about* Tarot) until I was at a festival in Charleston, SC one year and visited a used book vendor booth. Digging through the stack of New Age books I came across "Tarot for Writers" by Corrine Kenner and was ecstatic!

Being a writer of fiction as well, I knew that I had to have the book.

For anyone interested in how to use Tarot for character creation, plot outlines, story ideas, or creative writing prompts I highly recommend the book. I have only showcased a few ideas here to give people the initiative to use Tarot in a new and exciting way.

The saying "a picture is worth a thousand words" is so very true. One picture, no matter how complex or simple, can evoke different thoughts, ideas, feelings, emotions, and creative sparks.

Creative Writing students often have projects where they are given a picture to use as a prompt for story writing and some flash-fiction contests are based on a photo.

Using pictures as prompts are great activities that one can do just about anytime to eradicate writer's block, as writing exercises, classroom assignments or projects, and possibly even create something that gets published.

Tarot is a series of pictures that we already know tell their own story, that's how we read them in interpretations, and just like pictures in a magazine or from a camera they can be used as creative writing prompts.

Perhaps a person is just looking at the picture and describing the scene and conversation the people are having (things you may have already worked on in this book) or perhaps the cards are drawn in a way as to develop character or plot outlines.

Either way, using Tarot as writing prompts is a sure way to ignite the creative spark.

Character Creation

Think of a character you want to create; consider if they are an adult, a male or female, and perhaps their race or culture.

From that point on all of their strengths, weaknesses, traits, personality quirks, and such will be devised from the cards.

Write down different areas of a person's life such as: personality, work habits, political views, social life, morals or ethics, and so on.

Then, looking at each entry draw cards for that entry to get an idea of what the person is like.

For example, if writing about the character's work habits and you pull the Magician you might come up with the idea that he or she likes to, and always has, all of the right tools for the job. Draw as many cards as you need to get in-depth characteristics.

Fictional Characters

Take a look at your favorite movie, video game or book and choose your favorite, or least favorite, characters and then sort through a deck and choose cards that fit the character's personality.

This is not the same as the above example as you are not choosing cards to create a character but it is more like looking for querant cards for fictional characters.

Write or discuss why you chose that card and how it fits.

Tarot as a Focal Point

Write a story where the cards are a focal point, for example, I wrote a mystery-romance in which the main character uses Tarot cards in the beginning chapter to see how her vacation is going to pan out.

She also refers back to the reading several times throughout the story as she sees events tying in with the reading. When her room is ransacked and one of her cards goes missing, when she does find it she takes significance in the interpretation of the card when she does find it.

Tarot at a Party

Pretend the Major Arcana are all at a party, thinking of each card as a different personality type, (Moon would be a mysterious person, Sun a happy and bubbly person, etc.) write how all of them would react, behave or what they would say at the party.

Describe each card's "personality" at the party or the actions they would do, for example, the Fool might be the one who wears the stereotypical lampshade, drinks too much, passes out and gets his face drawn on by the others as he slumbers.

Brainstorming

Remember in school how we'd write a topic in a circle and then draw lines from it with key words or subtopics? For example, maybe

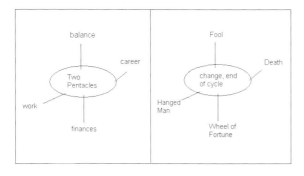

it was "octopus" and then words branching off from that may have been: habitat, life span, reproduction.

This can be done with Tarot cards by writing a card name in the bubble, then branches extending out for the key words. Another method to this is to write an idea and then branch off the cards that can be connected with it.

Poems, Songs or Raps

Draw three to five cards and write a poem or song using each card as inspiration for one stanza/refrain in the poem.

Or draw fifteen to twenty cards and use each card as inspiration for one line in the poem or song. Try also pulling cards just from the Minors, just from all of one suit, or just from the Majors.

Short Story

Select five to ten cards either by choice or at random and connect them by writing a short paragraph or story.

Remember to use the elemental, numerical, symbolism, and color correspondences you have already studied.

One-Card Short

Using just one card selected by choice or at random write a short paragraph or story about that card. Remember to use the elemental, numerical, symbolism, and color correspondences you have already studied.

Also consider what occurred just prior to or just after the scene in the card, what are we not seeing in the card but that aids in telling the story?

For example, in the Two of Pentacles we see a juggler. Maybe if we stretched this into a panoramic or looked at what he did that morning we see his wife and daughter with empty bowls, so he takes the one skill he has and tries to make money to feed them.

Panoramic

Sort through the deck and choose cards that look like they could be about similar events or that look like similar scenes. Piece them together like a puzzle (they won't match completely) by determining what happened first and so on; such as lining up all the cards with horses in them as if they are in a parade.

Or, use a "telescope" view and choose a card with a person, perhaps the Two of Wands, where a man is looking from a high vantage point, might see The Fool frolicking down below without a care in the world. Write a story involving these images.

Reversal Short Story

Select a few cards, either at random or by choice, and write a short paragraph or story based on their reversed meanings. Or, try mixing reversals and uprights and write a story involving those meanings.

The Fool's Journey

It is often said that the Major Arcana is the "Fool's Journey" as he travels through the cards and ends with the World.

The World is the end of a cycle with the understanding that the cycle repeats or a new cycle is about to begin.

I have seen several different sites in which the authors have written about the Major Arcana as if it is a journey of the Fool (Kim Huggen's Tarot 101 class at Witch School International does this).

With this in mind, write a story using all of the majors in ascending numerical order either starting with the Fool or any card desired.

If starting with a different Major card, continue in ascending or descending order (for example, if you draw the Empress, your next card for the storyline would be using the Emperor and you'd end with the High Priestess as the last card in the sequence or if going downwards start with Empress and go to The High Priestess, ending with the Emperor).

Write a Sentence

Randomly choose three to five cards and lay them in the order that they were drawn.

Look at the cards and write a complete sentence that encompasses the feelings or imagery in the card. Sentences can be literal and based on the scenes such as in the Hermit card: "a lone man walks with a lantern" or can be symbolic such as "a wise man searches for knowledge".

This exercise will also help you or can be combined with the entry on writing a key phrase for cards as seen in the sections for the Major and Minor Arcana.

Plot Outline

Choose or randomly select three to five cards to develop a plot outline. Look at the cards chosen and determine which things happens first and create a plot outline (based on imagination, not on numerical order). Perhaps the Fool sets out on an adventure, then meets a woman (Lovers) and they get married (two of cups), and have children (ten of cups).

Okay, so not the most elaborate of stories, but that's the basic concept.

As the story is being written, randomly draw another card and toss it into the mix to see how the story can change.

History of Tarot

Since the history of Tarot is ambiguous and steeped in mystery, create your own story about where Tarot came from or what its original purpose was.

But, don't take this activity seriously, make it fun and silly.

For example, maybe the very first Tarot deck ever was actually just pictures an alien child took with his camera while travelling the universe with his family. On their final stop on Earth he lost all his photos.

ABC's of Tarot

Write an ABC's of Tarot, using each letter of the alphabet write a sentence that coincides with something in Tarot such as "A is for advice, which the Tarot gives; B is for balance seen in the Two of Pentacles; C is for coins, sometimes called discs or diamonds" and so on until reaching the letter Z.

Different Imagery

Draw a card at random and write/discuss what other imagery could be used for that card (for example, the two of pentacles shows a man balancing/juggling two pentacles but could be represented perhaps by a man balancing on a tight rope or balance beam or balance could be represented by a set of scales).

Updating the Tarot

The images in Rider-Waite decks are from older eras as are images from other decks and there does not seem to be very man modern images.

Choose a few cards, concepts, or people depicted in the deck and update it to more modern day situations or people.

For example, the Hanged Man might be a bungee jumper or gymnast today and King's might be Presidents. Perhaps the chariot is public transportation or a racing competition.

Add a Card

Choose a favorite Tarot or Oracle deck and think about the cards that are in it. Now, consider what the deck may be lacking. Is there a card (or perhaps even a suit) that could be added to amplify the deck.

For example, in addition to pages, knights, queens and kings is there another distinction of royalty that would fit—perhaps in the courts the addition of a castle steward, chancellor, or maybe a royal advisor?

Deck Reviews

Do a review of several decks you own, write the review as if you are doing a book or movie review and not as an interpretation of the cards.

Books, layouts and spreads, websites, blogs, or Tarot classes can also be reviewed. There are many blog writers that do these very things and have faithful followers.

Try to make reviews at least 100 words. It is okay to not like a deck, but use constructive criticism in a review and write what is not likable and how it could have been better.

Book Reviews

Again, it is okay to not like a book as long as you can provide constructive criticism. Write a book review on any Tarot book for a journal, or discuss it in a group.

In fact, for group activities every member can bring a book and give an oral and informal review of it.

Reviews can also be posted at online sites such as Amazon, Barnes and Nobles, Good Reads, Epinions, message boards or blogs.

Cheat Sheet

Create a cheat sheet of card names, numerical correspondence, elemental correspondences, key words and key phrases.

This is good practice for remembering the meanings of the cards and if you have done the previous entries in other sections for writing your own key words and such then you already have all the information needed.

This can also be tucked in with a deck or your Tarot Kit and taken along for a quick glance during readings.

GROUP ACTIVITIES & GAMES

While many, if not all, of the prompts in this book can be adapted to group exercises, these next prompts are designed specifically for groups of people either as party-games or for Tarot study groups.

When I first created my own local Tarot group there was a mix of people who were long-time practitioners and beginners and I struggled to come up with activities that would be fun and educational and yet not be simple enough for beginners, but still meaningful to more experienced.

Those activities are seen in this section, with the addition of a few more that I created while writing this or had seen as examples on the internet.

Remember that in a Tarot group there may be wide diversity of those who are familiar with Tarot and those who have had no experiences at all.

While these activities are meant to help people learn about and become comfortable with Tarot they should also be taken lightly and as fun activities.

"Truth or Dare"

Use the cards almost as the "truth" part of the old slumber-party game "Truth or Dare" and ask questions such as "did so-n-so do this?" or "what is so-n-so thinking?" But, keep it light and fun and don't embarrass people or ask questions of a sensitive nature.

For example, a bunch of us women had gotten together and we had a friend being very secretive about a date the night before. So I asked the inevitable question of just *what* occurred on the date.

I phrased it in a yes/no question of "did they…" and the card I pulled was the Devil—you can imagine the laughter when I said "not only did they, but they used whips and chains!"

This wasn't a true interpretation of the card, but it made for some raucous giggling that day.

Round Robin Story

Shuffle the deck really well, then each person, in turn, draws one card and comes up with a sentence or short paragraph to describe an event, action, person, place or thing occurring in the story.

Each person adds to that story with the card they pull. Such as drawing the Two of Pentacles" there once was a juggler at the county fair…" then pass the deck to the next person and have them draw a card and add to the story.

Keep going until someone either can't come up with more to add to the story or the cards are all used up. Last person should try to use the last card in the deck to summarize or end the story.

Tarot Charades

Shuffle a deck of cards and fan them out face down. Have players pick a card at random and try to act out the scene. If you have costumes and props, use these for extra fun and to make it a little easier.

Tarot Win Lose or Draw

Play "Win Lose or Draw" ™ using Tarot cards as inspiration. Create teams of two or more people. Players randomly draw a card and then start drawing a picture depicting it (don't use words or numbers, only images).

A time limit of one minute is set and the drawer's team members try to guess what card it is; after the minute is up and they haven't guessed the opposing teams can try. One point goes to the team who guesses it right.

Tarot Fortunes

I saw this great activity online at "Yahoo Voices" by Sara Ganly. Place one Tarot card in an envelope for every person in attendance and set all the envelopes, mixed up, in the center of a table. Each person needs to go to the table and pick an envelope at random.

They will remove the card and on a piece of paper write a fortune (fortune-cookie style) on the paper but based on the images they see on the card. Place both the card and the paper back into the envelope.

When everyone is done, all envelopes will be put back onto the table, again mixed up. Then, each person goes up again and draws an envelope at random and shows off their card and reads their fortune.

Be as creative and fun as possible, again, a light-hearted or tongue-in-cheek approach should be taken when writing the fortunes so that everyone has a good laugh.

Tarot Group Deck

Gather several magazines and have everyone sit and look through them, cutting out pictures that can be used as Tarot cards. Glue pictures onto cardstock or index cards. Interpretations can be written as a group effort, or the cards can be divvied up and each person writes their own interpretations for the cards they were given.

Tarot Mix-Up

Cut out several pictures from magazines and glue on index cards (this part can also be a group project with everyone cutting out pictures or one person can set this up beforehand). Each person gets one card (if made beforehand shuffle and deal them out, one per person).

On a separate piece of paper each person writes an interpretation for their card without showing it anyone else. Then, gather the cards from everyone, mix them up, and lay them face up in a grid pattern on a flat surface.

Next, gather up all the interpretations and shuffle them up.

Then, give one to each person, making sure they do not get their own. Each person reads the interpretation they got and see if they can pick out the card it was written for.

Make sure players know to write an interpretation and not so much a description. For example, if they have a picture of a dog they need to write "a card of loyalty and friendship" rather than "a dog playing in a field."

This exercise can also be done with cards from Tarot deck, but is more of a challenge if using pictures from magazines as there are no universal messages pre-written for those.

Group Reading

Do a reading for the group (either as friends, a Tarot club, etc) using the Group Spread in this book (or one of your own). As a group, interpret the cards' meanings.

Ask questions such as a) what is group's purpose b) how do we see ourselves c) how do others see us d) what is our role in the community e) how can we make the group stronger.

Tarot Bingo

Find pictures of Tarot cards online from different decks and insert them into a five by five grid in a word document.

Remember to make it like Bingo in that not all of the cards in a deck will be on one Bingo Card and each Bingo card should be different.

A caller needs to be chosen and he or she will shuffle the deck and pull a card at random. Either name out the card as-is such as "High Priestess" or call out the meaning "she is a keeper of esoteric knowledge." Whoever gets a row either horizontal, diagonal, or vertical first wins.

There is a game I found at Dollar General called "Loteria" and is a sort of pictogram Bingo. There are 54 cards with images and a riddle.

On the Bingo cards are the same images, only sixteen of them, and the caller calls out the riddle on a card they have randomly selected from the deck. The players must cover whichever card image they think it is.

While it is not dubbed as being a Tarot deck, it has similar cards such as: Moon, the Sun, the World, Death, and Devil. But it also has animals such as heron and deer; objects; trees; and archetypes like gentleman or warrior.

The riddles are sometimes blatant such as the moon "the moon guides you at night." Sometimes they are poetic such as "it looks at God all day and lifts its arms to pray (tree)."

If you are lucky enough to find one I recommend it for personal or group use. You can also read more about Loteria on Wikipedia.

Play A Tarot Board Game

Never did I imagine there were Tarot board games until I received one from a friend. Since then I have also seen the Loteria game mentioned above as well as seen on Amazon one named the Tarot Game and created by Jude Alexander.

The one I got from my friend is called "The Mystic Circle" and was printed in South Australia by Zoix International Pty.

It is a board game with the spaces arranged in a circle and each space has an aura color, zodiac sign, element, or image of a Tarot card. Players toss the dice and travel around the board collecting cards. Spaces will ask players to choose a card, skip a turn, move ahead, or move to a specific square.

When a player has collected ten cards he or she stops. Remaining players continue until everyone has ten cards. The cards have no pictures, only the name and a reverse and upright meanings. The squares tell you to pick a card will tell you whether it's to be read upright or reversed.

When everyone has ten cards, they read them according to the Celtic Cross spread.

You can also create your own board game with large poster board and draw a winding path that fills up the board. Most spaces will be blank but have some that say "move ahead two," "take another turn" or "lose a turn" and have players roll dice. Some of the spaces can say "draw a card" and a person draws from the deck. At the end of the game each person has to read their cards as if doing a reading for themselves.

Or, another version of a game can be to have spaces name or show a picture of certain cards and when someone lands on it they will have to mention what key words, phrases, or interpretation they attribute it to it.

This makes players think about the cards and see how others

interpret them differently.

Songs & Movies Tarot

Choose five to ten songs, print off the lyrics or download the music and have each person pick a card that fits with the song; discuss why each person chose that card.

For movies, have each player choose their favorite movie and then select a Tarot card that fits that movie. Discuss why it is fitting and why you chose that card.

Tarot Match Game

Prior to this game write a brief description for each card such as "she is the keeper of knowledge and secrets." This game works best with a lot of people.

Divide the group in half and one half of the people get a Tarot card while the other half get a description (can be an interpretation, key words, sentence or maybe a riddle).

Players can talk and converse with each other to see who should be paired up. In the example given, does that description go with the High Priestess or Strength?

When everyone thinks they are paired up with their counterpart everyone divulges their card and description.

This can be done just as exercise in learning the cards or for points but then someone needs to keep a guide as to what description goes with what card, and be prepared for some debates on this since there may be more than one answer depending on a person's interpretation of a card.

Tarot Marriage

Prior to the game, pull all the cards that show only one person in it. If there are more people then there are cards you may want to use another deck or prior the game print pictures off the internet.

Each person draws a card at random from a stack and then will draw a number.

You will need two of the same number on different slips of paper, for example if there are ten people in the game you will need twenty slips of paper so you can have two number ones and so on.

The people with matching numbers get together. Their cards indicate their personality in the marriage.

Let's say Sue has Temperance and Bob has the Magician, they both draw the number three so Bob and Sue make a couple (do not worry if the couples end up as the same sex).

Now, the couple can draw a card from the remaining deck and this shows their future as a happily (or perhaps not!) married couple!

Tarot Crosswords and Word Searches

There are some great online sites that generate word searches and crosswords simply by putting in the words or clues you want. For crosswords consider clues such as "this card is of the earth element and means balance."

Or clues like "four of—" and based on the number of spaces or other letters connecting to it they will know if its cups, wands, etc.

Other clues could be "what number is the World card?"

Visit these websites for creating your own puzzles. www.crosswordpuzzlegames.com/create.html (crosswords) or www.armored penguin.com /wordsearch (word searches) or do a search online for other sites.

Tarot Quizzes

This can be done for fun at parties or as classroom quizzes to see how much people have learned or to see how well they have developed their interpretive skills.

Questions should range from "what does the Strength card mean?" or "what does the symbol of the sun represent in the Sun card?" or "what is the dog's meaning in the Fool card?" or "what symbols are in the Five of Wands card?" You can also describe scenes and the person has to answer what card it is.

Of course, for questions such as these each person will have to be using the same deck as even those that are Rider-Waite based will have variations.

Questions can be based on multiple choice, essay, fill-in-the-blank and be about numerical and elemental correspondences, symbols, the people, or anything else discussed in here. There are also several questions in this book that could be used.

Be creative but remember to keep it light and fun for party games or for classroom-type instructions remember that when it comes to interpretation, everyone's ideas are going to be different and the object of those questions is just to show that people are thinking.

For example, with the sun...if I write "it is symbolizing optimism and things are looking up" but someone else who is not a day person writes "it symbolizes things are too bright, they are too blinding and you cannot see the truth for being blinded by false happiness" neither answer is wrong.

But if someone writes "it means the sun is shining" well, this person is not putting a lot of thought into it.

TAROT & OTHER DIVINATION

Often, Tarot Readers also like to perform other types of divination as well.

Some of these can be combined for various reasons:

1) for it to help interpret the message of Tarot

2) for the Tarot cards to help interpret the meaning of other divination

3) to check divination skills (have one confirm the other)

4) to help enhance a reading or method of divination.

Many forms of divination such as tea leaf reading (tasseomancy) and candle wax scrying (ceromancy) use symbols in their divination. Shapes in the tea leaves or in the wax (hot wax poured into cold water) makes simple symbols or shapes and these are then interpreted.

But, often they are hard to discern and might look like blobs or might like different things to different people or from different angles.

Other forms such as crystal balls, scrying mirrors and scrying bowls rely on images or scenes that seem to play out before the diviner's eyes, but these can also be hard to interpret.

In this section I have included a few of the more common divination methods and how Tarot can be used as an aid. None of these are essential for a Tarot Reader to know and no one has to be psychic to perform any of these methods of divination.

If you are unfamiliar with the different methods below there are books, You Tube videos, and websites that farther explain what they are or instructions for how to use them.

If there are other divination methods that you like to use, think of ways that you can incorporate Tarot into them.

Tarot and Runes

Granted, Runes and Tarot don't always mix but I have seen Rune sets that came with colorful cards depicting scenes, symbols or situations that tie in with the Rune's meanings.

It was devised to give a more mental image to the querant's who have a hard time visualizing things.

They could also be used as a learning tool for studying the Runes. Someone who is studying both can look at the meanings of Runes and pull out cards that fit the same meaning.

Tarot and Pendulums

Pendulums are fascinating objects which have use both in metaphysical and scientific realms.

In Tarot they can be used to corroborate a reading by asking such questions as "does this card mean—?" and observing the answer the pendulum indicates.

Some people always use clockwise as yes and counter-clockwise as no but I have had pendulums that do not sway in circles but rather side-to-side or back and forth, so I prefer to ask the pendulum which ways are yes and no.

Hold it still and say "show me yes," observe which direction it turns. Then, ask it to "show me no" and observe that direction.

Another method is to think of a question and at least two possible answers/outcomes.

Choose cards that depict these outcomes and place in an arc. Ask the question while holding the pendulum, the card it sways to is the answer.

Cleansing cards can also be done with a pendulum. Either set the deck down neatly stacked, or spread the cards over a large surface such as a table. Hold the pendulum over the cards and ask it to cleanse the deck. It will start spinning, when it stops consider the deck cleansed.

If you've spread the cards over a large area you may have to move the pendulum to different areas in order for it to hover over all the cards.

Tarot and Scrying

Often the images scene in scrying either in a crystal ball, scrying mirror or bowl, or candle wax poured into cold water can be difficult to discern.

When trying these methods you can also pick one Tarot card at random to help decipher the images seen in scrying by randomly selecting a card after shuffling and cutting the deck.

Think of the same question asked for the scrying and ask it again of Tarot or think of the image seen in scrying and ask Tarot what message that image was trying to convey.

Tarot and Dreams

I have found that since I started studying Tarot I often dream of it. I have had several dreams where I am either doing a reading or I am seeing cards in the dream.

Always there is one or two that sticks out very prominently, sometimes it is an actual Tarot card and sometimes a made-up dream Tarot card, for example I dreamt of a Tarot deck with an image of a ship on rough seas at night.

The picture was on a Tarot card but not in any deck I own in the waking world. If you dream of Tarot, decipher it the same as in a regular reading.

For other dreams you have had that you are certain have meaning but are having a hard time interpreting, use Tarot to clarify the messages.

Think of the dream and ask what message it was trying to convey.

Then after shuffling and cutting the deck select three cards at random and read those as an interpretation to your dream.

Tarot and Spirit Boards

Using Tarot with Spirit Boards (or Ouija Boards) can be used similar to how a pendulum is used by using the Tarot images to replace the traditional letters and numbers on a Spirit Board.

Place ten cards face up in an arc, place fingers lightly on a planchett (the pointers that come with Ouija boards; a small, overturned glass; or a smooth, polished and large stone work well).

Ask a question and the card that the planchett moves to is your answer (of course you still have to interpret the card's meaning).

If it does not go towards any of the cards, place those cards aside and pull ten more.

You could also use Spirit Boards to interpret cards or a reading by asking what message the cards are trying to convey. The Spirit Board will, literally, spell out a message.

Tarot Bibliomancy

Bibliomancy is a form of divination in which a person opens a book at random and divines an answer from the text within.

For Tarot Bibliomancy you will need your journal where you have written interpretations about the cards, or a Tarot book that has card interpretations.

Ask a question and open the book at random. The card you opened it to divines your answer. If there is more than one card on a page or pages that are back to back (meaning the left side is one card and the right is another card) then close your eyes before opening and point somewhere on a page, then open your eyes.

Tarot Fortune Cookies

Okay, so this isn't a serious form of divination but it is fun. And I don't know anyone who doesn't read their fortune in a cookie.

For a fun activity, we can use these little quips of wisdom with Tarot. When you get a fortune cookie, read it and then think about what Tarot card it most likely resembles.

For example, a fortune that says "you have all the tools and knowledge you need to get ahead" might be connected with the Magician card.

Another idea is to use the lucky numbers on the back in a reading using the majors.

For every number there, pull that card from the Major Arcana and read them together to determine what the fortune is trying to say or what your future will be.

For numbers on a fortune cookie fortune that are higher then the Major Arcana goes, such as 42, reduce it to a single digit.

WHAT YOU HAVE LEARNED

After you have spent a good amount of time learning how to use Tarot cards and have done several activities in this book, take some time to look at these questions and either think about the answers, write them in your journal, or discuss them in a group activity.

Three Things You Have Learned

Thinking on everything you have learned from Tarot or this book, pick out three things that are the most important to you or that had the most meaning to you.

You can also choose three activities (or even sections) that were the most helpful to you or you had the most fun with.

Three Things Others Need to Know

Write or discuss at least three things that you want others to know or realize about Tarot.

For example do you want others to be aware of the myths and why they are myths, or perhaps it's to bring about awareness of how useful Tarot cards can be in our daily lives.

Personal Value

Think about why Tarot is important to you and answer the following questions: Why were you interested in learning Tarot? How has, or how do you think it will enhance and benefit your life? How do you think you will use it (reading only for others, daily draws, reading it only when needed, for meditation, in spells, etc)?

The Hardest to Learn

What were or are three things that have been the hardest to learn, or what goals have been the hardest to achieve? (For me its understanding and interpreting the Court Cards.)

Apprehensions or Misgivings

What misgivings or apprehensions did you have when you first started practicing or studying Tarot? How did you get over those in order to continue your pursuit of Tarot?

Myths

Think about some of the myths you have heard or use the examples given in this book. Why do you think these myths exist? What other myths have you heard of? Has you concern over these myths been alleviated with this book or through studying Tarot?

What Has This Book Taught You?

After you have finished reading this book and have done several activities in it has it helped you as an individual or a group? How did you use this book and what is your opinion of it?

OTHER IDEAS

The following ideas are a little more involved and require knowledge or actions that go behind just buying and reading a Tarot deck but all can be beneficial in learning and connecting to Tarot.

When it comes to the entries involving writing a book, creating videos, websites, or writing newsletters and blogs keep in mind that proper citations must be met.

If unfamiliar with citing sources and information I suggest looking it up in a respectable writing how-to book or taking a writing course.

Posting pictures of cards in decks can also lead to copyright infringement and often companies will only give you permission to post a few cards.

Don't take it lightly when creating any written or recorded media; there is a proper way and an improper way. That being said, my little disclaimer to the world, here are my final ideas for connecting or learning about Tarot.

Join or Create an Online Group or Blog

Sharing with others, even if online, is an excellent way to learn and enhance Tarot skills, ask questions, and to share reviews of decks.

There are several great member sites out there already with information, deck reviews, and forums.

Blogs are just informational and even though comments can be made it is generally not interactive like a group or message board. But, with blogs the followers will get text or email updates when a new message is posted.

Aeclectic Tarot (www.aeclectic.net) is a wonderful site with a message group, and Tarotholics Anonymous on Facebook is another good one.

Do a search on the internet or Facebook for more groups or blogs and join one that appeals to you; if there isn't any that suit you, then perhaps it is time to create your own.

Tarot & the Internet

There are various Tarot-related pages on Twitter and Facebook that offer inspirational messages, daily readings, and other fun stuff. Facebook also has a Social Tarot app that is like a game where you get readings and offer readings (all computer-generated) to other people and collect points, etc.

I followed a Twitter account once that posted a card and a brief meaning daily. I don't have any real recommendations here, but search "Tarot" in Twitter or Facebook.

Create an Offline Group

A group that meets in person is a great way to learn about Tarot and to teach it to others. Our group met once a month and we usually have either pot luck or the home owner where we met at would cook. We'd spend about three hours laughing, talking, and learning about Tarot. Base the studies on the group's needs.

As I have said before, my group had both beginners and experienced so I had to gear activities and studies towards that. At the first meeting ask people their level of experience and what they need to work on or what they want to learn.

Creating a group on Café Mom, Facebook, or Meet-up.com is a great way to make it localized (put the area in the title or select 'regional' in group settings) and make sure it is mentioned that this group meets offline.

The online group can be used to discuss meetings, post information and create events.

Complete an Online Class

There are several online classes for Tarot, some require payment and some do not. There is a free Tarot class that comes in the form of an email from About.Com offered by Patty Wigington (see bibliography).

I took part in an extremely good course titled Tarot 101 offered at Witch School International and written by Kim Huggens (see bibliography).

Grey School of Wizardry also offers a course on Tarot

(www.greyschool.com).

The American Tarot Association (www.ata-tarot.com) and the World Metaphysical Association (www.worldmeta.org/tarotcert.htm) also offer tier-level courses, you have to complete certain steps and requirements to move onto the next level, and each level costs you.

At the end of some these courses or classes you get a certificate, however, Tarot is not an accredited career or course of study such as welding, child care, nursing, massage therapy, etc. and there are no standard or universal rules, laws, or regulations concerning it and what one needs to do to be a Tarot Reader. But the courses are helpful in learning Tarot, building confidence, and giving you a sense of accomplishment.

So, the online courses while fun, entertaining and educational will not really make you a certified Tarot Reader and the certificate is only worth the paper it is printed on and a personal sense of accomplishment.

To perform Tarot as a business all you need is a general business license, but there is no accreditation for being a Tarot Reader.

Collect More Decks!

I have not come across a Tarot reader or enthusiast yet who has only one deck.

Collecting decks can be rewarding and fun, even if only a few of them are used for readings. Having more than one deck gives you something to barter or trade with, a different deck can give different insight into a reading, querant's can choose which deck they are most comfortable with (and this can say something about the querant) and collecting decks is just, well, its fun!

It's like collecting unicorn figurines, antique furniture, or Pokémon cards. It is fun, we like to collect the things we like and we like Tarot cards! Keep an eye out for them everywhere, I have gotten decks at Michaels Arts and

Guest Speakers or Workshops

Pagan groups, Renaissance fairs, spiritual festivals, and other such events enjoy having people come in and do readings either as a vendor, or as a workshop or guest lecturer.

Look around for events in your area (Witch Vox is a great site to find events) and contact event coordinators to see if they'd be willing to have you come. Most lectures or workshops last about thirty-minutes so have enough material to cover the time span, make it interesting, and offer something to the guests in return.

At one such workshop the host printed off pictures of the court cards and each person drew a card, she then explained what it meant about them (their personality type).

Be honest to event coordinators about how many years of experience you have and don't attempt to do this if you just started studying recently as you may come off as sounding inexperienced (which you are) and giving guests the wrong ideas about Tarot.

As a vendor you would have to comply with whatever regulations the event coordinators set up and discern which type of reading you will do, how long each session is and what you will charge. In some states you may be required to have a business license as you will be charging for a service.

Watch or Create Tarot Videos

There are some great Tarot videos online at You Tube. Do a search in the site's search engine and view a couple different videos. Take notes on things you want to remember, favorite or share the videos, or write a critique of the person's knowledge or methods in the video. Perhaps try making your own video and upload it to You Tube to share with others.

Trade or Sell

Often Tarot card collectors will sell or trade decks that they no longer want. Amazon and EBay are great places to sell decks or books and Etsy is a great place to sell Tarot-related handmade items.

Message boards are also great places to post decks for sale or trade (but check with the guidelines of moderators or administrators first).

If there are enough people in an offline group set up a Tarot Trade and everyone gets together to trade decks equally and amicably.

Decks can also be given to others as gifts.

Create a Syllabus for Your Own Studies

As I have said before, my own pursuits in studying Tarot has led to this book's creation and one of the first things I did was create a list of things I wanted to accomplish in Tarot. I didn't place dates with it, it was simply a list of what I wanted to study or do first.

For example, I had "study one Major Arcana every day". I started with the Fool and read up on what he meant in two or three different books, I took notes, and then I wrote down what my own observations or interpretations were.

Also on my "syllabus" were items such as learn three new spreads really well, study the court cards, write three Tarot Spreads, and do a Daily Draw everyday for a month.

Using this book or ideas you may come up with on your own, write a goal list or syllabus of things you definitely want to accomplish as you study and learn about Tarot.

This activity can be done for those just learning about Tarot or for the more experienced. Don't attempt to include everything from this book on your list, but do include at least ten items you want to accomplish within a certain time period.

For example "I will write key words for all of the cards in three months time."

Once those items have been accomplished you can go back and choose some other ideas from this book.

Remember, this book is not to be done every day for a year but rather it simply just includes 365 different activities. It is up to each student to decide what they want to do, when and how.

Create Your Own 365 List!

And, finally, create a personal list of 365 journal prompts, spells, meditation, activities learning exercises, and creative writing prompts that can be done with Tarot. But, be warned, it is not as easy as it looks!

Bonus Challenges

So, you have now read through 365 different prompts and activities that, in reality, equals a lot more when you take into consideration some of the prompts have you working with more than one spread or one card and some have multiple questions to answer in each entry..

Technically, you can consider the prompt about writing key words for the majors as twenty-one different prompts or activities. But, as I said before this book is not meant to be done for every day of the year or even in a year's time, it is just 365 because it is a nice number to shoot for.

But, just in case I didn't give you enough to do here are a few more ideas I decided to throw in at the last minute. Have fun!

21-Card Spread

Reading twenty-one cards is a challenge but can give quite a detailed reading and for complicated issues it may be just the layout to use in order to sort things out or put them into perspective. This is like a Past-Present-Future spread but there are seven cards to represent each aspect.

There are also other spreads in books and the internet that involve twenty-one cards such as "The Complete Book of Tarot Spreads" in which each position has a different meaning.

This spread can be laid out in three rows of seven and then it would be read the same as any past-present-future spread but incorporate all seven cards into the reading for that time allocation.

However, it could also be done in a Pyramid Spread with each row indicating something different, or it could be done in seven rows of three with each row indicating a different aspect of life such as: work, physical, play, romance, health, home, and the self.

The Clock Spread

This is another spread written by me with inspiration from one of my favorite solitaire games. This is a challenge in that is reads twelve cards. This card uses the numerical correspondences for its positions.

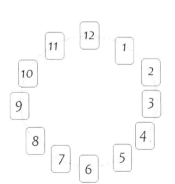

1)SELF: the person as an individual, this can be a card randomly chosen or can be a querant card.

2) BALANCE: what the Querant needs to balance in their life.

3) TRINITY: this spot is the person's religious or spiritual affinities or what they need to work on spiritually.

4) STABILITY: this card represents what is important to the person, what they need in order to feel stable in life

5) PRESENT: represents the present moment or situation because the present is neither the future nor the past. It can also indicate what challenges are at present.

6) FUTURE: what the potential outcome of a situation may be or where the person is headed.

7) MYSTICISM: this is your inner secrets, mysticism, meditation, or intuition and what you need to know in order to tap into these or utilize these skills.

8) KARMA: indicates a karmic loop you are stuck in (a bad pattern that you repeat) or what rewards from good karmic behavior that you may be reaping (or will reap).

9) END OF CYCLE: represents the end of a cycle, something that is ending to make room for the new.

10) NEW BEGINNINGS: the beginning of a new

11) THE PAST: your past and what regrets we have in it, things that are holding us back from our desired outcome.

12) FINAL OUTCOME: indicates the final outcome of our situation or question based on the cards in the other numbered slots.

Do 50 Free Readings

While I was studying Tarot I had a friend who was studying Massage Therapy and one of her criteria was to give fifty free massages and then her clients signed off on a sheet and critiqued her.

I thought "what a wonderful idea!"

So, for anyone who wants to start doing this as a business, for strangers, for trade or at fairs and festivals I recommend doing fifty readings for free for friends prior to setting this up as a practice whether for business or fairs.

Have your Querants give you feedback or even complete surveys so you know have some idea of what is good or want needs to be changed.

To make it easy, you can let one person receive two readings so really only need twenty-five people (this is what the massage school did.)

Two-Person Spreads © Kalista Anderson

As far as I know my daughter Kalista invented this concept when she was twelve years old. She is one of the best Tarot readers and writer of new spreads that I know; I have even seen her use Pokémon cards in a reading.

She came up with a two-person spread one afternoon and we tried it out for fun. They actually work great and are perfect for friends or couples to get.

The first one shows the connection between two people, and the second is for two people who need to resolve a conflict.

Both parties should be at the reading and give their permission as it is unethical to do 3rd party readings (reading for someone not present) or to read for someone who doesn't want one.

The spreads are like the Basic Spread and are mirror images of each other with an extra card tucked in the middle to connect the two.

Readers can read both the #1 positions for each person and flip-flop back and forth to read all positions, ending at the middle card and tying the two readings together.

Or, readers can read one side (1-4) and then read the other side and then connect the two readings. The circles of ABC are simply where people sit with A and B being the two querant's and C being the reader.

Version One:

This spread can be just a general reading or with a specific question in mind.

1 & 6) WHOLE SELF: this is the person as a whole, their desires and dreams, wishes and goals, and their personality. It is a summary of their self.

2 & 7) PAST: this is their past influences, what led them to this point or what is holding them back.

3 & 8) PRESENT: the current situation; what is currently at hand; the problem, situation or question.

4 & 9) FUTURE: future outcomes and endeavors, what will occur based on the decisions at the moment, what the person needs to be on the lookout for later or how they can resolve the

situation or achieve their desire.

5) THE RELATIONSHIP: the relationship or connection between the two people. It may be an emotional connection, physical, business, or other connection. It may indicate conflicts or success they have had or what binds them together.

Version Two:

This spread is specifically for resolving a problem that is occurring between the two people.

1 & 6) NEEDS: what the person(s) need to do for themselves for this situation.

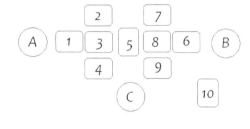

2 & 7) PAST: past influences, feelings or emotions that are holding them back and blocking them from resolution.

3 & 8) PRESENT: present influences, attitudes or emotions that are affecting the situation right now

4 & 9) FUTURE: future attitudes or effects on the person if the situation is not resolved

5) SITUATION AT HAND: what is going on and how it affects the two people as a whole, or how the couple can resolve their differences.

10) FINAL OUTCOME: the final outcome if the situation is not resolved. A bonus card can be drawn to show what the

outcome will be if the situation is resolved.

Write Interpretations for EVERY Card

If you didn't already do this as part of the past exercises, take the time to write a brief interpretation for every card in a chosen deck.

Don't forget to write key words, phrases, and brief summary of what it means. You can also include color, symbol, reversed, and numerical meanings.

More Concepts

Here are dozens of more concepts that you can pull one or two cards for at random to see what Tarot says about it or why we need it, its purpose, etc. Or, go through the deck and choose cards that aptly fit these concepts the best

Emotions: love, hate, grief, depression, loneliness, happiness, sadness, disrespect, sorrow, excitement, apprehension, anxiety, anticipation, apathy, laughter, anger, jealousy, irritation, upset, pride.

Events: theft, illness, birth/pregnancy, buying a home, graduation, empty nest syndrome, career change, change in residence, court situations or legal matters, celebration, natural disasters, solitude, financial difficulties or bankruptcy, financial security.

Life Cycles or Relationships: growing old, childhood memories, children, siblings, marriage, unwanted divorce, anniversaries, breaking up, family or friends,

Inner Qualities: forgiveness, chivalry, honesty, leadership, transformation, spirituality, trust, respect, success, inner strength,

Write a Book!

In addition to creating their own deck, many Tarot enthusiasts have written books. Remember to cite your sources!

Publish a Deck

Keep in mind that if you are using a deck of internet images or clip-art it cannot be published. You also cannot publish a deck on a copyrighted theme such as from TV, songs or movies.

If there isn't a Star Trek theme you can't make one and publish it without permission from the creators of Star Trek. However, your own theme, photos and drawings you can publish.

With photos you often need permission from the people in the photo or the owners of the building. Check online for submission guidelines before submitting a deck for publication.

AUTHOR'S END NOTE

I hope that by the end of this book you have found some activities you would like to try (or have tried) and that they have been helpful to you in creating a lesson-plan for yourself, for teaching others, or just for fun projects that help you connect with the Tarot.

While I have done many of the activities in here I have not done them all but I do plan on sitting down and working through many more activities or prompts.

I would also love to hear from readers who have done some of these activities and whether it worked well or didn't as well as constructive criticism about how to make the ideas better or other things to include.

If you made an art or craft related to Tarot, please send me pictures. My website and Facebook addresses are in my Author Bio and I would love to hear from readers.

Additionally, if you have reviewed the book or are interested in reviewing it please let me know so I can read it and post a link to it on my website. I have enjoyed writing this book and hope that readers enjoy it as well and get a lot of use out of it.

APPENDIXES

After much deliberation I have decided to include a few appendixes including a glossary and correspondences to numbers, elements, animals, zodiac signs, symbols, and colors.

I have, however, not included key words, phrases, or interpretations for the Major or Minor Arcana because part of the aim of this book is to use the exercises in it to come up with your own. Plus, there are hundreds of books already delving into the meanings of individual cards.

Another reason is that even though I wrote it based on Rider Waite decks, other decks may be used with this book. And, other decks have different imagery or have different meanings. This goes the same for Oracle decks.

I also did not include individual animals in the appendixes because there are just too many to name. I highly recommend buying Ted Andrews "Animal Speak" book which is the most comprehensive animal book I am familiar with.

I also have not included individual flower or herb names for the same reason. Cunninghamn's Encyclopedia of Magical Herbs is an excellent resource to learn the correspondences of plants, or you can search for the Victorian Language of Flowers on the internet for meanings to flowers and herbaceous plants.

NUMERICAL CORRESPONDENCES

In New Age, Pagan, and Wiccan practices correspondences are attached only to the numbers 0-9 typically speaking, however 11-13 do have correspondences based on superstitions, folklore, and in some religious contexts so I have included those in here as well.

Since Minor Arcana do not go above ten in the numerical sycle and the numbers with the Major Arcana are not used in conjunction with the card's meanings we do not need to delve into the higher numbers.

However, numbers are all around us and we can attach our own personal correspondences to them.

Zero

Because of its shape, zero indicates cycles which have no true beginning or ending. We see this in the Fool card in the Major Arcana.

He is at the beginning of a journey, but when we have reached the end of the journey with the World we cycle back around to becoming the Fool again about to set of on a new beginning and so forth.

One

The true beginning of the numerical cycle this is a number of beginnings, prime forces individuality, alone or loneliness, uniqueness and the self. It is the ultimate reality, a source for all existence and the basis for all numbers.

Two

This is a number signifying duality, balance, togetherness, the yin-yang, complete opposites or opposing forces, relationships and couples.

Two is prominent in religion in that it was the number of every animal Noah brought onto the ark, it is the number of stone tablets the commandments were written on, and two candles are often used on altars in various religions to ring in a Sabbat or Holy Day.

In Wicca there are two candles (at least) to represent the masculine or god energies and the feminine or goddess energies.

Three

This is a number that means growth and represents several different forms of trinities or holy triads in a variety of belief systems. It also can represent the tripartite male genitals and the triangular female genitals.

Three also plays prominently in superstitions and is either seen as good or bad depending on the source. Some say "bad things happen in threes" and yet others say "third time is the charm."   In Wicca three is seen as a powerful number for spells and rituals.

The world is seen as having three dimensions and this is a number of synchronicity when we consider that we often do things on the count of three (on the count of three, let's all push this heavy great, for example).

Four

This is the archetypal family of four, stability, the four elements, the four seasons, the four winds or directions, and a number of manifestations. It is a number that plays prominently in Buddhism, Hinduism, Judeo-Christian and Islamic beliefs.

Five

The number five has a lot of correspondences such as the five senses, the shape of the human form (head, arms, and legs), five fingers and toes, the five points on a star, and in come cultures five elements (such as water, wood, metal, earth and fire) or the four elements plus spirit.

It is the middle of a cycle and represents the present because it is neither here nor there. In the numerical scale of 1-9 it is dead-center. Because it is in the center it can also represent confusion or uncertainty (should it go forward or backward).

Six

This is a number of harmony, choices, decisions, cooperation, creation, equilibrium and equal forces. This numbers is often thought of as a perfect number as well (twelve is another perfect number).

Seven

Often thought of as a spiritual or mystical number it is one of good luck and spiritual introspection. It is an active force and a heavenly number.

It has prominence in Judeo-Christian, Hindu and Islamic religions as a lucky or divine number.

In Japan there are seven lucky gods, sometimes known as the seven gods of fortune. It also denotes the days of the week.

Eight

Balance, achievement, material accomplishment and manifestations this is a number that resembles the infinity sign of which there is no beginning and no ending. It is a number of power, and similar in shape to the infinity sign.

There are eight Sabbats in the Wiccan wheel, eight spokes on the Buddhist wheel, and in Hinduism it is a sign of wealth and abundance.

Nine

The last single digit in the numerical cycle, this number is the end of a cycle or phase. It is a number of completion, success and wisdom. The number nine is a good number in Chinese cultures and is associated with the Chinese dragon which is a symbol of magic and power.

Ten

This is the first of the two-digit numbers and one that has both the numbers one and zero in them indicating the beginning (one) of a new cycle (zero). It is a number of changes and fortune.

Eleven

Often seen as good luck number and there is a common superstition that to make a wish when seeing the number 11:11 on a digital clock will guarantee the wish comes true.

Twelve

Twelve is considered a perfect number and one of high status in mythology as there were twelve disciples of Christ, twelve labors of Hercules, there are twelve months in a year, twelve animals in the Chinese zodiac, and twelve signs in the Greco-Roman zodiac.

Twelve is also a dozen of anything which is deemed as the perfect amount.

Thirteen

If twelve is a perfect number than adding on to it is surely bad luck. To have thirteen of anything is said to tempt the fate of the gods and bring about curses and bad luck. It was believed that thirteen was a sign of the Devil and that witches (of the folklore and misguided stereotypes of centuries ago) numbered thirteen in covens.

Evens

Even numbers are thought of as balanced and equal and are numbers exactly divisible by two. They are a sign of equilibrium, stability, the Yin, femininity and the answer no. A lot of evens or all even numbers in a Tarot read may indicate the answer is no or a negative outcome.

Odds

Odd numbers are forceful, the Yang, masculine and portray a positive outcome or the answer yes. They are a sign of opposing forces or "odd man out." A lot of odds or all odd numbers in a Tarot read may indicate the answer is yes or a positive outcome.

Elemental & Suit Correspondences

As stated earlier, some readers may place fire with wands (both indicate energy) and air with swords (ceremonial symbolism).

I have always done the opposite because I think of bladed items being forged in fire and wands being waved in air (stage magician wand, a conductor's baton, etc). And for the purpose of this book, this how I have placed them.

Please adjust according to your beliefs or viewpoints.

Earth & Pentacles

Earth is our mundane and physical world; it is our health, jobs, career, finances, our home, material possessions, and our physical needs.

It is often represented by rocks, dirt, salt, or plants or symbolized with pentacles, diamonds, discs, or coins when used in Tarot. In some Pagan practices it is seen as a working element so any tool that you work with, such as bolline or a cauldron, might also be used for earth.

It is the direction of North and is represented by earth-tone colors such as green or brown. It is a grounding force and one of stability, comfort, and protection. Earth is associated with gnomes as its elemental.

People who feel a kinship with this element tend to work with their hands, they may be gardeners, woodworkers, or people who work outdoors or in the fields of wildlife or horticulture.

In Tarot, the merchant trade is represented by earth.

Water & Cups

Water is a free-flowing substance that takes many forms and adapts to the shape and form of the container it is in. giving us the concept that we need to be flexible and have a "go with the flow" attitude about certain things.

It is an element of motherhood, birth, renewal, rejuvenation, free-thinking, femininity. emotions and sometimes creativity. It is considered live-giving and because we spend the first nine months of our life in fluid in the womb it is seen as birth and motherhood.

It is the emotional realm and in a Poker deck it is seen as hearts because hearts are connected with emotions and their shape resembles goblets or cups. Water is in the direction of west and associated with blues and greens.

It is also represented with cups, cauldrons, goblets, bowls, or any other vessel that holds water. On an altar it is symbolized with a chalice or bowl of water, seashells, or sea critters. It is associated with the elemental of undines.

People who feel a kinship with this element might enjoy water sports or work with water such as in marine science, water quality, fishermen, sailors, or other trades.

In Tarot it is clergy or religious leaders and represents emotions.

Fire & Swords

Fire is symbolic of energy or action and swords also show action and signify those who do battle with their trade position being that of knights or soldiers.

Fire is represented by the colors red, orange or yellow and the direction of south. It can be represented by the elemental creatures known as salamanders or even dragons. On an altar fire would be represented by candles.

Fire is the intellectual realm; it is passion, zest, and motivation. It is represented by swords, which in Tarot represents piercing, pricking, and points (making a point) and associated with soldiers, knights or anyone in battle. Sometimes other bladed instruments are seen in Tarot such as athames, bollines, knives, daggers or spades.

People who feel a kinship with the fire element might be ones who enjoy action and seeing results. A "do this, and that happens" type of attitude such as we see in making fire. You add fuel, oxygen and an ignition source and you see results (fire).

In Tarot it might mean action, energy, a go get-'em attitude, communication, conflict, or strife.

Air & Wands

Air is often confused with water because they both have similar properties in that they take the form of whatever vessel they are in, are free-flowing, and undulating.

Air is the direction of East and represented by the colors of white, gray or yellow and the elementals known as sylphs. The trade of wands is seen as laborers or farmers.

Air is symbolized by wands which are sometimes seen as staves, sticks, rods, or batons. Air is spiritual or intangible concepts that we can neither see nor hear but we feel or experience.

In Tarot it is a sign of spirituality or inner reflection.

ZODIAC CORRESPONDENCES

Reading signs of the zodiac in Tarot can be done in several ways: the reader can interpret the sign as being either the querant, someone involved in the querant's life or just the generally feeling of the card.

For example, if a sign of Aries (either the symbol or an image of a ram) shows up in a card it might just mean the positive influences such as adventure and a pioneering attitude (or the negative traits if reversed) rather than represent an actual person.

Meaning, that person might have to 'adopt' the qualities of that sign in order to get their desired results.

When looking at patterns in the cards look for animals or objects that can be representations of the signs such as in the Strength card there is a picture of a lion (Leo) or in the Moon card there is a scorpion (Scorpio).

Or, the astrological symbol (seen next to each entry) might be depicted in the card.

Aries (Mar 21—Apr 19)♈

Represented by a ram and of the fire element, Aries' positive traits are adventurous, energetic, pioneering, courageous, enthusiasm, confidence, dynamic, and quick-witted. Its negative traits ar: selfish, quick-tempered, impulsive, impatient, foolish, and a daredevil.

Taurus (April 20—May 20) ♉

Taurus is represented by the symbol of a bull and is of the earth element. Its positive traits are patience, reliability, warm hearted, a loving attitude, persistence, determination, and security. Its negative traits are jealousy, possessiveness, resentful nature, inflexibility, self-indulgence and greed.

Gemini (May 21—June 20) ♊

Seen as a sign of the twins and an air element, Gemini has positive characteristics including adaptability, versatility, communication, wit, intellect, eloquence, and a youthful and lively personality. In the negative, it is seen as someone nervous, tense, superficial, inconsistent, cunning and inquisitive to a point of being nosy.

Cancer (June 21—July 22) ♋

A water sign represented by the crab, Cancer people are emotional but loving, intuitive, imaginative, sometimes shrewd and cautious, protective and sympathetic to others feelings and emotions. In the negative, they are moody and apt to change moods or attitudes quickly, overemotional, touch, and clinging often not wanting to let go whether it is emotional attachment or attachment to materialist things.

Leo (July 23—Aug 22) ♌

Leo is a fire sign and like the lion it is named for it is a sign of strength and endurance but also one of generosity, warm-heartedness, and a broad-minded person who is faithful and loving. Its negative aspects are of pompousness, patronizing, bossy or interfering, sometimes dogmatic and intolerant.

Virgo (Aug 23—Sept 22) ♍

An earth sign, Virgo is known as the Virgins and is a sign of modesty, shyness, meticulousness, reliability, practicality, diligence and an intelligent or analytical mind. But, it can also be sign of someone who is fussy, a worrier, overcritical to the point of being harsh, and someone who is a perfectionist or conservative.

Libra (Sept 23—Oct 22) ♎

The scales, often a symbol of balance, represent the Libra sign. It is an air sign and is one of diplomacy, romance, being sociable or easy-going, idealism and peace. Its negative traits are indecision, gullibility, someone who is easily influenced, self-indulgence and flirtatious behaviors.

Scorpio (Oct 23—Nov 21) ♏

Scorpio, or the Scorpion, is a water sign and shows someone who is determined, forceful, emotional, intuitive, powerful, passionate, exciting and has a magnetic personality. Its negative qualities are of someone who is jealous, resentful, compulsive, obsessive, and may be secretive and obstinate.

Sagittarius (Nov 21—Dec 21) ♐

Sagittarius is the sign of the Archer and is a fire sign. It is one of optimism, freedom, a jovial or good-humored person, and someone who is honest, straightforward, or philosophical. Negative traits attached to this symbol may include a person who is blindly optimistic, often missing or ignoring the bad news even when laid out before them, and someone who might be careless, irresponsible, has no tact, or someone who is superficial.

Capricorn (Dec 22—Jan 19) ♑

Capricorns are represented by the goat and are an earth sign with the positive traits being one of practicality, prudence, ambition or discipline. A person born under this sign may also be one with great patience, always careful and has a good sense of humor, even if a little reserved at times. Less favorable traits of this personality type may include pessimism or a fatalistic attitude and someone who is miserly or holds grudges.

Aquarius (Jan 20—Feb 18) ≈

The water bearer, Aquarius is actually an air sign and anyone born under this sign might be one who is friendly and a good humanitarian. They are probably loyal and honest, maybe even to a fault, and show great intellect and independence. On the reverse side, they may be unpredictable people who have a perverse sense of pleasure, are contradictory, and may be emotionally detached.

Pisces (Feb 18—Mar 20) ♓

Pisces are a water sign and symbolized by fish. People with this sign use their imagination and may be sensitive, compassionate and kind. They are generally selfless and not drawn to materialism. On a negative side, they may want to escape from reality, are secretive or vague, and may be weak-willed and easily led into temptations.

COLOR CORRESPONDENCES

Like with all things, there are personal and universal correspondences to colors and in addition to being used in color magick, the use of colors has its place in therapy and psychological studies.

Colors denote feelings and moods in us and are very powerful.

Incorporating the color of an object from a card into a reading is very useful and the colors used can give great insight into what the artist was trying to convey.

Black

Black is a color with a bad reputation of representing evil, bad luck, sin, violence, death and evil. However, it can also be used to indicate darkness, power, secrets and magic. When seen in clothing it usually denotes sophistication and elegance.

Blue

Blue is considered a cool color and represents ice, water, the sky, winter, and the cold. It also represents sadness such as in the saying "feeling blue" but it is also a color of calming influences, magic and truth. It is a color used for baby boys and also was commonly used for police or royalty.

Brown

Often ignored for being thought of as a drab color, brown is a color of stability, grounding, humility, and indigenous people or things. It is also a color of earth, soil, nature and wood.

Green

Green is a color most often used to represent recycling, nature or the environmental movement. But it is also a color of health, growth, movement, luck, money, hope, and youthfulness. It also has pessimistic traits such as sickness, greed, envy and inexperience.

Grey

Another "drab" color grey, or gray, is often overlooked but it can be a color to indicate neutrality and contentment. However, it typically has less desirous traits such as pessimism, depression, blandness or boredom, old age, something that is undefined, and either foggy or stormy weather. Because it is the color of ashes it also signifies mourning and repentance.

Metal Colors (gold, silver, copper, and bronze)

These colors represent wealth, money, riches, prosperity,

finances, and abundance. Gold also represents a male deity or the sun and silver is a color of the moon and female deities.

Orange

Another warm color, orange typically means luck or creativity in Paganism but it is also a color to indicate amusement, unconventional, and activity. It, like the color red, is used as a warning or danger (think of orange road construction signs or cones) and can also indicate something is important.

It can mean determination, desire, compassion, endurance and optimism. It is an important and sacred color in Buddhist and Hindu practices. It can also be used to represent fire.

Pink

Basically just a lighter hue of red, pink is often used in the same concepts as its darker counterpart. However, pink does have its own defining qualities such as being used for baby girls and also used to represent the dawn, awareness, calmness, a color representing fairies, beauty, cuteness, glamour and friendship,

Purple

If pink is a color of the dawn then purple is the twilight color. It is also a color of royalty, piety, nobility, religion, faith and spiritual awareness. In candle magic it is a color used to heighten one's sense or psychic powers. It is also a color of vanity, strength wealth and privilege.

Red

Considered a "warm" color, red typically is a color used for danger or as a warning. We also think of it as a color of anger because of the popular concept of seeing red when angry. It is also a color of fire, heat, and energy.

Because our blood and hearts are red it is the color used most often for health, hearts, life, and blood. It also can be used to indicate passion, beauty, seduction and sexuality.

In some cultures it is seen as a color happiness, immortality, force, sacrifice and martyrs.

White

When all else fails, go with white whether it is in clothing, house or room colors, or candle magic.

White is an all-purpose color and one of piety, innocence, perfection, goodness, loyalty, honesty, cleanliness, newness, neutrality or surrendering, light, nobility, emptiness, protection, angels, heaven, snow, peace, life and sterility.

It is a color of softness, freshness, and purity and basically an all-around positive color. It is often a color used to represent deities on an altar, often used for a female deity when a silver candle is not available.

Yellow

Yellow is a happy color that represents sunshine, summertime, pleasure, warmth, hope and fun. In some instances it can mean reason, optimism, friendship, hope and imagination. Adversely it can mean jealousy, envy, betrayal, cowardice, warning, caution, and to go slow. It is also a color used to indicate electricity or fire and can be used to a male deity on an altar if a gold candle is not available.

COMMON SYMBOLS & THEIR MEANING

The following is just an overview of some basic symbols that might be seen in a Tarot deck. I have lumped together some items that all have the same meaning such as letters or phones being under the heading for communication devices.

Remember, there may be symbols in a card or deck not listed here and that everything in a card is important and can be used in interpretation.

Anchors

Just as they were deigned for, anchors are a symbol of holding something in place or holding your position on something. It is something that is dependable, reliable, provides stability and is used to secure something.

Angels

Angels, cherubs, or any deity figure in a Tarot card is going to signify divine or spiritual guidance. It may also indicate that the querant may need to go on a vision quest or use meditation to get the answer they seek or resolve the problem.

Animals

All animals will have individual correspondences attached to them as well as elemental correspondences. But, in general terms animals are a symbol of habits and instincts because that is what they rely on.

Breaking it down further, you can look at domestic animals (cows, chickens, etc) as being a symbol of hard work or sustenance. Household pets are a sign of contentment and companionship.

Exotic animals could be interpreted as travel or something that is unique or foreign.

Animals can also be broken down into the elements and all birds would be air; desert animals are of fire; water animals of water; and land animals as earth.

So, even if you do not know individual correspondences an animal in a card can still be interpreted.

Artistic Implements

Artist pallets, easels, typewriters, writing, pens, paper or anything that is used for arts, crafts or writing may indicate that a person should be utilizing their artistic talents (or are ignoring them, depending on the reading) or that they may need to look at situation with a new perspective. It could also mean that they need to find a creative or imaginative solution.

Baby

A baby in a Tarot card is almost always a sign of innocence, a new idea or concept (the 'birth' of a new idea), and union or partnership. Babies have a fresh outlook on life and they are also the result of a couple uniting and are almost always a positive sign, but do not necessarily predict pregnancy or birth.

Bells

Bells are of the air element (because they ring) and can be seen as signs of communication because they are used to ring out the dinner hour and were used to call servants in a mansion or as doorbells.

Bells are often used to announce the approach of something, such as the time in a clock or churches summoning people to service. They are also warnings, signals, and musical instruments. The sound of bells is also believed to summon fairies and scare off spirits.

Books

Books of any kind indicate wisdom or knowledge in a Tarot card. A closed book might mean that the person is ignoring what they are being told or already know or it can indicate a person is "like a closed book" and keeps things to them selves.

An open book means that the answers are right there in front of you or can indicate that a person is "like an open book" and it is easy to read their emotions or personality.

The type of book can also indicate an answer such as a

handyman or cook book might mean that the querant needs to use practical knowledge or common sense whereas a religious book might mean to seek religious or spiritual advice.

Bow and Arrow

Because they are weapons and made for hunting a bow and arrow can represent both sustenance and providing for one's family as well as protection. But they also represent skill and the ability to hit a target.

An arrow in a target may mean the person is on track with their goals whereas a bow and arrow being ignored might represent ignoring what needs to be done to reach a goal.

Bridges

These are connectors between one thing and another and represent transitions. This might be a transition in physical life, moving from one place to another, or moving from one career to another. Bridges can also be signs of a transition on a metaphysical aspect. They are also supports that help us make these transitions.

Buildings

When seeing buildings in a card think of what the purpose is of that building in order to incorporate it into an interpretation.

Castles would represent protection, strength or fortitude; homes represent stability, solidarity, family; banks are signs of financial matters; businesses represent careers or jobs; churches are symbols of a spiritual or religious matter; and schools are signs of education, learning or knowledge.

Caduceus

A staff with two snakes entwined around it, the caduceus was a symbol of both Hermes and Asclepius of Greek mythology and of Mercury in Roman mythology.

Asclepius is the Greek god of healing so the symbol has come to mean healing or the medical field and is often seen in hospitals and is used by the US Army Medical Corp.

In a Tarot card it means the same, and may indicate a person needs to be concerned with their physical health or pay attention to it.

A caduceus is also a sign of balance, union or even opposing forces.

Candles, Lanterns, Flashlights, Torches

As objects that light our way in the dark these implements mean to shed light on a situation in a Tarot card. If the lights are off or extinguished it could mean we have lost our way.

The old man in the Hermit card typically carries a lantern as if he is searching for something. In a metaphysical sense, these devices can represent light (such as 'seeing the light'), life and spirituality.

Chains

Chains are often a representation of obstacles or things holding you back.

As seen in the Devil card, the people wearing the chains are ignoring the fact that the chains are loose enough to slip off and be free, making this card a message that someone has self-imposed bonds.

These are obligations, restrictions, or obstacles we place on ourselves and that are often unneeded. Chains can also be a sign that someone is feeling trapped or bound to something not of their choosing.

Circles or Triangles

Most geometric shapes do not have much significance in a Tarot deck unless the deck is based solely on symbols or shapes. But circles and triangles typically always have some meaning.

Circles basically stand for cycles such as the seasons, the cycle of life, phases of a person's growth and development or of never-ending processes.

Triangles, once believed to be a divine shape, will mean divinity or any triple deity it holy trinity implications. The reason walking under ladders is considered bad luck is because when leaned up against a wall it forms a triangle, which is a divine shape, and to walk through that space would anger the gods.

Clocks, Calendars, Sundials, Hourglasses

Anything that shows the passage of time indicates just that, or might be showing us scheduling conflicts or that it is time to make schedules and be more organized. Combine this with numerical references for any number that might be on the calendar or on clock to get an even deeper meaning. These items can also show cycles.

Clothing

As discussed earlier, clothing can be a clear indication of the meaning of a card.

Fancy clothing shows wealth, riches or being conscientious about appearances whereas shabby clothing shows either poverty, lack of a materialistic attitude, or not caring about appearances.

Hats, veils or baggy and loose clothing that hides the body may indicate shame, hiding or secrets, or being self-conscious. Ceremonial or ritual clothing may indicate spiritual guidance or advice.

Columns

These are supports for buildings, arches and bridges and represent fortitude, stability, and constancy. They are pillars of strength but they work together, meaning that you can't have one column holding up an entire building but instead you need several in order for the supports to work.

Communication Devices

Objects such as phones, letters, billboards, scrolls, and even carrier pigeons are all signs of communication and may indicate that a message is going to be received or that a message needs to be given to someone. For example, if you have been holding back on telling someone something then the time might have come to reveal that.

Compass, Maps

Compasses and maps give us direction and keep us from getting lost. They let us know where we are in the world and in a card can indicate that we are on the right track. However, if a character in the card is looking at one and looks puzzled it could mean he has lost his way.

Cornucopia or Baskets of Food

These items indicate harvest, prosperity and abundance. They are the rewards reaped after a hard labor. Items such as a refrigerator, grocery store, pantry, or gardens and crops can indicate the same. However, the baskets or pantries are empty and the crops dead it indicates the opposite. In a reversed card a basket or food may indicate you are about to lose all of your abundance and prosperity if you are not careful (food will fall out of an upturned basket).

Crown, Coronet

Crowns are a sign of royal, seigniorial, or papal authority and prestige. They might also be a sign of victory, especially if seen as a laurel wreath or coronet. They mean someone has reached the pinnacle of something (sports, career position, authority, etc). However, a crown of thorns such as seen in the crucifixion of Christ is a sign of adversity and sacrifice.

Flags

Flags of any type can mean patriotism, loyalty, victory, or travel. Flags that are triangular such as pennants or wind socks may also indicate a direction such as "time to move forward" or "time to reflect on the past for your answer." If a flag is of one's own country it may mean patriotism whereas a flag for another country would mean travel.

Flowers or Wreaths

Each flower has its own meaning so if there is a flower, such as rose, that stands out and is easily discernible then the meaning can be interpreted along with other symbols in the card.

But, flowers, just in general, can be a sign of gift-giving (especially as seen in the Six of Cups where a boy is giving a young girl flowers), beauty, truth and innocence.

Flowers in a garden may indicate it is time to develop a hobby that is peaceful or may indicate it is time to slow down and take time to "stop and smell the flowers."

Wreaths, depending on the scene, can indicate victory or congratulations but if the scene is one of a funeral or death then they represent sorrow or grief.

Food Items

Similar to the cornucopia, food items of any kind will represent harvest, abundance, prosperity or sustenance. If the food is being given to someone of shared with a group it can represent socialization and sharing what you have.

Someone who is hoarding food would mean just that; the person is selfish or depending on the reading it might indicate that it is time to stop being selfish. Food items can also stand for knowledge or nourishment (in a literal sense, such as nourishment of the mind).

Globes, The World

Any image of a world or globe can indicate having 'the whole world at hand,' in other words: many opportunities. In the Two of Wands a man literally holds a globe in his hand as he oversees the land—a sure sign of success.

Good Luck Symbols

Good luck symbols such as four-leaf clovers, horseshoes, stars, or other such symbols will indicate good luck.

In a reversed card they can indicate that good luck has run out or bad luck is on the way.

Depending on the size of the symbol or its prominence in the picture can indicate how much good luck is coming (a lot verses just a little).

Hearts

Hearts are going to represent love, emotions, or health. Pay attention to the color of the heart or its status. A broken heart will indicate that emotions or feelings have been hurt, poor health, or that a relationship has broken apart. Hearts are also symbols of cups or chalices.

Infinity Symbol

The infinity symbol, which looks like a sideways eight, is a sign of everlasting, eternity, infinity, long-life or something that is cyclic and has no beginnings and no endings.

Jewelry, Diamonds, Money, Gold

Anything of value is going to represent materialism, wealth, abundance, career options, promotions, success or prosperity. In an opposite aspect, an empty wallet or treasure chest may indicate a person needs to be wary lest they go broke.

Seeing people gamble or gambling implements can mean either the time is opportune to make gambles or take chances, or that it is not wise to do either (depending on where the card is in a layout).

Seeing scales of money or someone juggling money such as the Two of Pentacles may mean it is time to balance the finances and budget.

Lists

If a card denotes a list or someone writing a list it can mean that it is time to prioritize, make an agenda or get organized in order to get the desired results or get ahead with a project or in a job.

Moon

There is a moon card in Tarot but it may also appear in other cards. The moon represents mystery, secrets, far-off plans and represents feminine concepts such as female deities or monthly feminine cycles.

It also represents nocturnal animals, such as wolves, cycles, and perhaps that things need to be done in "darkness" or covertly.

If the moon is large and prominent it can mean that secrets are about to be revealed whereas a small moon may mean that these things are far off from being known.

The triple moon, a full moon surrounded by two crescents, indicates the Triple God and Goddess aspects seen in some Pagan practices.

The left crescent is the maiden or lad; the full moon is the mother/father or sometimes seen as the hero; and the right crescent is the crone or sage.

Musical Instruments

Typically, musical instruments will mean festivities, happiness, celebration, hobbies, or careers in music. If the instruments are being played it is a time of celebration but if the instruments are neglected it may mean that someone is ignoring their skills or that the time for celebration either has not come or is already gone.

Nudity

Nudity in a card is often a sign of vulnerability or naiveté. It can also mean openness and that the person has nothing to hide.

Depending on the card and its position in a layout it could mean a person has no shame or humility but if the person is shown as cowering or trying to cover up it can mean the opposite. Nudity is also symbolic of honesty.

Opposites

Anytime you see any opposites in a card it means balance. For example, in the High Priestess of Rider-Waite decks we see a black column and white column which are polar opposites and means balance or opposing forces. The Chariot of RWS decks also does this with a black sphinx and a white sphinx drawing the chariot.

Peace Symbols

Any symbol that typically represents peace such as doves, olive branches, the peace sign done with fingers, or the hippie peace symbol all represent peace, calmness, contentment, etc.

However, if a reversed card is used it could indicate that peace needs to be found before their can be any resolution.

Radio, Television

Both of these can also be correspondences to communication but they are also signs of receiving information, entertainment, or the broadcasting of knowledge.

Look at the status of the object in a card; if it is off or being ignored it could mean messages are not being received, a broken one might mean there are obstacles preventing communication or information from coming through or if a radio or TV are on and the character is watching it and ignoring what is going on behind them it may mean it is time to ease up on entertainment and pay attention to more important matters.

Rainbow

In Christian lore the rainbow was God's promise to the people that he would never flood the earth again as he did in Noah's time. Because of this it has come to mean a sign of promises or hope.

Because the colors of the Chakra (centers of spiritual power in the body) are seen in a rainbow it may also indicate that a person's Chakras are all aligned and in tune.

In Greek mythology Iris is a messenger goddess who uses the rainbow to travel back and forth delivering messages between man and god, so it can also represent messages in a Tarot card.

Religious Texts or Symbols

Anything of religious status can mean that divine intervention such as prayer, meditation, inner reflection, or spiritual awareness needs to be met or is at hand.

They can also mean that someone might need to seek the advice of a clergyman, shaman, elder, or priest/priestess for guidance. If someone is looking at a religious career choice this card may be giving the go-ahead.

Roads and Road Signs

Roads show us direction in life or can be signs of travel or goals. A road or path that diverges shows decisions need to be made or a road that simply ends could indicate that a person's journey has come to an end.

A road that is "beat-up" and doesn't look well-traveled may mean it is time to follow the path less travelled (meaning to take an option that is not common or obvious).

In real life road signs direct, warn, guide and inform us so in a fortune-telling card decks they do the same.

Directional arrows or signs may indicate that the person either needs to look to the future or remember something from the past.

Stop signs would mean to cease certain activities and yield or caution signs can mean to go slow or be careful with a situation.

Scales

Scales almost always indicate balance, juggling, or budgeting but they also may mean weighing both sides of a situation before making judgment, such as listing the pros and cons of each side.

Seeds

Seeds or seedlings are a symbol of growth, rebirth or cycles. They can also be seen as a symbol of fertility.

Seeing someone toss seeds onto the ground might indicate someone will soon reap what they have sown or that it is time to cast out seeds (set things in motion) in order to reap benefits or rewards (for example, it might be a prime time to mail out resumes or book proposals).

Shepherd's Hook

Because shepherds watch over their flock, the hook or crook they carry is a sign of watchfulness.

However, these items are often seen in religious imagery and even in the depiction of the Grim Reaper and they can also mean faith, pastoral authority, or that someone has jurisdiction over something.

If seen coming in sideways to a scene and not being held by someone it could also mean getting rid of something unfavorable, such as in the old time Vaudeville scenes where the bad performer is pulled off stage with a crook.

Stars

Aside from meaning good luck stars also indicate reaching for the stars (success), fame, and wishes being granted. They only come out at night so it may mean that sometimes we have to wait for other secrets or knowledge (nighttime) to come about before we can see other aspects of the situation.

Sun

The sun is a sign of the god aspect and also indicates seeing the light of a situation, seeing clearly, optimism, bright futures or situations, happiness, and just generally very positive qualities.

However, keep in mind that it can have negative associations as well and may mean a person is blinded from seeing the truth.

A small sun may indicate that they are far removed from happiness or optimism and may need to find both in order to proceed.

A sun that is showing people thirsty or crops wilting may indicate a person is too optimistic or has too much fun and doesn't see the reality of the situation or what it is doing to them or the things and people around them.

Telescope, Binoculars, Spyglass

Anything that is used to look at something far away can indicate that while the future outcome is still far off, it is not inconceivable and can still 'be seen,' that is to say it is in the realm of possibilities.

These items give us an overview of the future or something far away and help us to see it more clearly.

Toys

These are signs of the past, of our youth and our childhood innocence.

Depending on how the rest of the card reads with other imagery or in the layout they can either mean it is time to let go of our childhood and start being more mature or they can mean we may need to remember the fun and innocence we had has children and try to hold onto that.

Games are a sign of our perspective on life, think of the

concepts of games: team playing, solitary (some card games or online games), searching (hide-n-seek), catching something (tag), or competition (board games), strategy or mental dexterity (chess).

Utensils or Tools

The Magician card has all the tools of the elements on his table and his card means having all the "tools" or knowledge you need to proceed. Tools in other cards can mean the same.

Any tool or household implement will mean we need tools in some form to accomplish something or may mean that the answer or solution is a physical one and one we have to work for it. An example might be getting a job: they don't just fall into one's lap but you have to fill out applications, create resumes, go to business, etc.

Vehicles

Forward motion, competing or competition (if more than one vehicle) or travel are presented by vehicles of any kind.

Depending on where the vehicle is can also indicate what type of "travel" or "forward motion."

For example, boats can indicate we are moving forward with our emotions or airplanes would mean moving forward with communication.

Vehicles that are stranded or stuck would indicate that we are stuck in a rut and unable to move forward.

Water

We know that the suit of cups is a water element but sometimes water shows up in other cards as well.

Aside from being emotions water can also mean travel (if seen in oceans, lakes and rivers) or if someone is in water or being rained on it can indicate a cleansing or a consecration such as a Baptism or a Wiccaning.

Water being poured may indicate someone poured out or is about to pour out their emotions and cups overflowing may mean their emotions are taking over the situation.

Stormy seas, as already stated, indicate anger or turbulent emotions or situations.

Weapons

Any item that can be considered a weapon or implement of battle such as armor, shields, catapults, etc can indicate a battle of sorts.

It may be a battle of wills, an internal struggle, or a fight with people. It may be fighting something in courts or trying to get justice out of a situation.

The weapons might indicate that you either have or need the right tools for the right job. Such as going into court you need documentation and proof of the injustices served and to have all your facts straight.

Weather and Seasons

When reading the cards pay attention to the weather or seasons depicted in each one (if possible—some cards may not indicate this). Storms, storm clouds or rough waters indicate emotionally or physically turbulent times.

Clear skies or smooth waters mean peaceful times.

Aside from the elemental correspondences, the seasons also indicate stages of development and concepts.

Spring is youth, renewal, rebirth, an emergence of something, and growth.

Summer is young adult, happiness, success, fulfillment of life, and increased activity.

Fall or autumn is the mature adult and a sign of harvests, late maturity (such as in projects) or even the development of something that follows it most vigorous phase just before the decline.

Winter is old age and a sign of wisdom, inactivity, a time of hibernation or endings or something that is declining.

Wheels

These are a symbol of innovation, invention, direction, fortune, travel, trials, and forward motion.

We see wheels on vehicles, as gears, or in games of chance (wheel of fortune) but regardless of what they are used for they have no movement of their own and will just sit there useless until someone or something moves them.

Either we are moving the wheels by hand or we use engines to make them move. Wheels show us that without some sort of action, there will be no forward movement or progression.

Windows, Doors

Windows and doors often mean opportunity. If there are windows it might mean that the opportunity is right there before the person—they can *see* it—like we see through a window, but they are not yet able to reach it because of an obstacle.

Open doors represent opportunity is at hand whereas a closed door might represent that while opportunities exist they are not close at hand right now. A lot of windows or doors in a scene, such as a hallway, might indicate that there are many choices available right now.

TOOLS TO ENHANCE A TAROT READING

As mentioned earlier, tools can be used to enhance a reading either because of the qualities they inherently have, by opening up our chakra centers, or simply by creating ambience.

Gemstone, candle, aroma, and color therapies are common in New Age, Wiccan, Pagan, and Metaphysical practices.

For the following items, there are numerous correspondences but for the purposes of this section I am only including the correspondences that tie into the purpose of enhancing a reading.

For example, a yellow candle also represents male deities, hope, jealousy, and many other aspects but for this section I have only written to use a yellow candle for communication or concentration as those two things tie into a reading.

This section is for tools only used for readings and to set the right mood or ambience or to open up channels of intuition and psychic or spiritual awareness.

A wonderful source for looking up correspondences of herbs, colors, oils, gemstones, and incense is "The Magickal Cat" (see

Bibliography for URL).

Bells

Bells are said to be used for communication, as signals, and to cleanse an area of evil spirits (they don't like noise).

To cleanse an area before a reading ring a bill several times while walking around the space, or ring the bell three times over a deck of cards to cleanse it.

A bell can also be rung just before the reading to signal its start, and right after a reading to signal its end.

Candles

Candles led an air of ambience because they provide a low and comfortable atmosphere.

Be careful as it is an open flame and should never be left unattended or placed too close to flammables.

Colors to think about for enhancing a reading are: black for grounding or enhance scrying abilities; blue or brown for communication; yellow for communication and concentration; purple for opening psychic channels, divination, and spiritual guidance; white for purity, cleansing, all-purpose, and spirituality; gold for divination; light blue for spirituality; or silver for psychic awareness and intuition.

"Creature Comforts"

Of course, all parties involved in the reading should be

comfortable meaning the room temperature should be comfortable, chairs or seating areas comfortable, and neither party should be inebriated in any fashion.

Many readers will not even attempt a reading if they are sick or at all feeling under the weather as it can take personal energy to do a reading.

Other things to consider are whether the area is private, public, or semi-private. Can the querant here what you are saying? If you are outside is the wind going to blow away your cards? Is it too dark to see the cards? Do you have enough time to read for them?

No one wants to be rushed through a reading and not get their full money's worth (even if they are not paying, they want a decent and accurate reading).

Gemstones

Gemstones can be stored with cards to enhance the card's energies and they can be set up around the Tarot cards when doing a reading. A practitioner can also wear certain gemstones or hold one in her hand (a querant can also hold a gemstone).

Additionally, a reader can place their birthstone with the cards to add a sense of personal energy to the deck.

It is believed that gemstones and crystals have an energy all their own and that by being near them we are picking up and benefiting from that energy.

Gemstones to consider are: snowflake obsidian for grounding, absorbing negativity, and spiritual energy; clear quartz for psychic powers; onyx for scrying; sapphire for meditation and improving communication; obsidian for grounding; centering, and divination; malachite for scrying, opening 3rd eye, divination and enhance psychic abilities; moonstone for spiritual understanding; lepidalite for clear communication; labradorite, jet, or lapis lazuli for divination; kyanite for medication, communication and cleansing; chalcedony for reducing negativity (from a negative querant); chyrsophase for sharpening perception; sodalite for improving communication; amber for cleansing and positive energy; amethyst for increasing spiritual awareness; emerald for psychic awareness, meditation and divination; and hematite for divination, grounding, and scrying.

Herbs or Smudge Sticks

Herbs can be sprinkled on the surface of the table, the floor, burned, placed in water bottles and spritzed around the room, or fresh herbs can be bundled together and dipped in blessed water (or water and fragrance oil mix) and the room or area asperged (flick the bundle to let the water droplets fly off to cleanse an area).

Herbs can also be sprinkled over decks or in deck boxes to cleanse or consecrate them. Again, if burning herbs get permission from the querant first.

A few herbs to try are: alder for divination; yarrow for divination and opening psychic channels; white sage for purification and cleansing; lemon grass for a psychic cleansing or opening channels; myrrh for spiritual openness, meditation, and high psychic vibrations; dandelion root for divination; calendula flowers for psychic and spiritual powers; and mugwort stored with a deck to increase its powers of divination.

Incense

Incense is inexpensive as are the burners for them, and they come in such a variety of aromas that anyone's sense will be pleased. However, just like when using candles some people may not want incense burned depending on allergies, asthma or just personal preference. Always ask first.

If they agree, then you can use an incense of choice but if you have a variety you can ask the querant which incense they prefer. Incense is bought in sticks or cones and both are equal, however cones and burners for cone incense tend to be more compact to carry in a Tarot Kit.

The smell of incense can cause an ambience of comfort and relaxation which may be necessary to get a good reading.

Some choice incense might be: sage for purifying and cleansing; frankincense for creating a sacred space and consecrating objects; honeysuckle for psychic powers; lotus for meditation and opening the mind's eye; cedar for purification; lilac for powers of clairvoyance; and sandalwood for psychic powers.

Oils

Oils can be placed in oil burners for the same effect as incense and may be a better choice if a person is asthmatic and the smoke will affect them. There is a wide variety of both fragrance and essential oils that can be used, fragrance oils are often sold near candles in department stores at an inexpensive price.

Fragrance oils are artificial scents whereas essential oils are 100% pure plant extracts. For the purposes listed here either one works fine, but essential oils are recommended when it comes to homeopathic remedies.

Oils can also be used to anoint the cards, the reader, a Tarot cloth, or the querant or can be placed in a spritzer with water and sprayed over or around an area to cleanse it or add its properties.

Again, ask the querant if he or she minds being anointed as sensitive skin may break out.

Oils should always be stored in blue, green, or amber bottles at room temperature and away from sunlight to maintain their potency.

Oils to consider are: wood aloes for spirituality; clove for divination; tea tree for cleansing; benison to awaken the conscious mind; chamomile for meditation; lemon grass for psychic awareness; and sandalwood for spirituality or meditation.

Music

We all know that music sets certain moods: for romance, for sleeping, for parties, to enhance a movie, or to put us in that holiday spirit. Music can also enhance a reading in that it adds another element of calmness and relaxation.

I recommend New Age or Instrumental music (classical such as Beethoven or Mozart work great) as anything with words might subconsciously alter the reader's interpretations of the cards.

Strings of Beads

Some of your querant's may be getting a reading for the first time and will be nervous. Hand them a string of beads to keep them from fidgeting. Any beads will work, but one that has interesting shapes or trinkets on it might be tactilely pleasing and ones made of gemstones will give them the energy of the stones. If a querant seems nervous offer them a string of beads to toy with as a focused way of fidgeting.

GLOSSARY

Ace(s)

In Poker decks this is a playing card that has a single mark on it with a value of 'one.' In Poker decks it is typically represented with the letter A. In Tarot this is also a value of 'one' and means "new beginnings."

Arcana

Means secrets or mysteries; the 'arcana' is either one of two groups of cards in Tarot decks; the major arcana (or trumps) and the minor arcana (suits).

Archetype, Archetypal

Carl Jung first coined these terms during his studies to describe images, personality or experiences that tend to be common among all of mankind. The archetypal family (or stereotypical) is a man, a wife, and two kids.

In Tarot archetypes are used often such as the Emperor is an archetype of leadership or the four of wands is an archetype for the 'traditional and happy family.'

Bonus Cards

Extra cards in a reading that can reveal hidden meanings, clarify cards or the reading, show alternative outcomes or add something to the reading.

Card Readers

People who read cards as a means of telling the future, also known as cartomancy (the act of) or cartomancers (those who read cards).

Cartomancy

A term used to describe the method of fortune-telling using a deck of cards; from Latin with the suffix meaning 'to see.' People who practice cartomancy are known as cartomancers.

Celtic Cross

A popular spread for Tarot cards that comes in many guidebooks accompanying decks and involves either seven to nine cards. It is used to give a 'big picture' overview of a person's situation or of their life.

This spread was discovered by Waite in the early 1900's and is said to represent the bridge between Heaven and Earth. Typically ten cards are used.

Clarification Cards

'Bonus cards' that may be used in a reading to clarify the meaning of a card or spread.

Cleanse

To rid an object or person of unwanted or negative energies.

Code of Ethics

A written code indicating the rights or the reader and the querant which also may include disclaimers of what Tarot can and cannot do or the popular disclaimer "for entertainment purposes only."

Consecrate

To dedicate something to a particular purpose; to bless or making something sacred.

Court Cards

Suited, non-trump card depicting a person or persons as seen in a royal court; there are four cards in each suit or element that typically includes Page, Knight, Queen and King although other alternatives are seen depending on the deck. Court cards depict personalities or people in the querant's life.

Craft

Any art, skill, trade or occupation; Tarot is often referred to as a craft.

Disclaimer

A statement renouncing legal right or to free someone from damages or liabilities whether legal, psychological, financial or medical.

Divination

The act of seeking knowledge through supernatural or otherworldly means; the method or practice of foretelling the future or discovering the unknown through omens, oracles, or supernatural powers; the prophecy of prediction. It is derived from the Latin word *divinus* meaning "to be inspired by the Gods."

Elements (The Four Elements)

A concept seen in Pagan and New Age practices but dating back to the ancient Greek philosophical movement and typically seen as earth, air, water and fire; also known as the basic archai in philosophical terms.

Esoteric: Secret knowledge or knowledge that is hidden away from the general public typically is meant to be shared with only a select few. It is believed that the Tarot contains esoteric, or secret messages that we, as readers, are interpreting.

Hierophant

A term used for someone who interprets and explains obscure or mysterious matters, especially sacred doctrines. The Hierophant card in the Major Arcana is often seen as the High Priest, which essentially is the same thing.

Kabbalah (Qabbalah)

Terms used to define a discipline or 'school of thought' involving ancient Judaism or Jewish mysticism.

Layout

A spread of Tarot cards, typically each position in a layout has a specific meaning and the cards may be set in a particular order and in a particular pattern. See also 'spread.'

Major Arcana

One of two groups in a Tarot deck made up of twenty-two cards numbered zero through twenty one; means "big secrets" and is typically thought to represent the spiritual realm; also known as trumps or triumph cards.

Major Arcana depict people or things in an allegorical context and a are powerful cards that have very spiritual and powerful meanings

.

Minor Arcana

One of two groups in a Tarot deck made up of pips and court

cards; the pips are 1-10 and the courts are typically Page, Knight, Queen and King; there are four suits based on the four elements making for fifty-six cards total; means "little secrets."

Oracle Deck

Any deck that does fit within the standard Rider-Waite system involving four suits with Pips and Courts and with a fifth "suit" known as the Major Arcana.

Oracle decks typically do not have the seventy-eight cards as seen in Rider-Waite based decks but may have as few as twenty or as many as eighty. They are still fortune-telling cards and using them is still known as cartomancy.

Pendulum

Any weight on a string used in divination to determine the answers to yes/no or binary questions.

Pip Cards

Cards numbered 1-10 that along with the court cards help to make the Minor Arcana; there are four sets of pips in a Tarot deck.

Poker Decks

A standard set of playing cards with four suits of diamonds and hearts (red cards) and spades and clubs (black cards). Poker decks are used for a variety of card playing games.

Positions

The placement of the cards in a spread or layout. In most spreads the positions mean different things and are used in conjunction with the card meaning and the querant's question in order to divine a meaning.

Power Card

A card representing the querant in a Tarot Reading.

Querant

The person asking the question, or who the reading is for which can be yourself or someone else.

Querant Card

A card representing the querant in a Tarot Reading.

Reading

The process of revealing the cards meaning to the querant

Reversals

A term used when the cards are randomly placed and read in a deck upside down. Using reversals changes the meaning of the card.

Rider Waite Decks

Sometimes referred to as Rider-Waite-Smith, Waite-Smith or

Rider-Waite-Coleman-Smith, and just the Rider deck; often abbreviated as RW or RWS. This is the first mass-produced and most popular of Tarot decks in English speaking countries.

The images depict Christian, Catholic, Freemason, and esoteric imagery in a style of the Renaissance era. The illustrations were done by Pamela Coleman-Smith (1878-1951) and the deck created by Arthur Edward Waite (1857-1942) and the deck published by the Rider Company.

The deck was first published in 1909 and was the first complete deck of seventy-eight cards and the longest running deck still in publication today.

Runes

These are letters from several ancient and Germanic alphabets used before the widespread adoption of the Roman alphabet (circa 3rd and 13th centuries). But can also be used to identify any magical symbol or inscription.

Today runes are used in spells or in divination and are written or etched on pieces of glass, bone, stone or wood with the Norse Futhark Runes being the most common.

Significator Card

Another term used for a card representing the querant in a Tarot Reading.

Spirit Board

Sometimes referred to as Angel Boards, Talking Boards or Ouija. This is a board with letters laid out in an arc or circle and users place their fingers on a pointer or upturned glass and ask questions. Spirits or unseen forces guide the object to the letters to spell out an answer.

Spread

A layout of Tarot cards, typically each position in a layout has a specific meaning and the cards may be set in a particular order and in a particular pattern; also known as 'layout.'

Standard Deck

A standard set of playing cards with four suits of diamonds and hearts (red cards) and spades and clubs (black cards). Standard decks are used for a variety of card playing games; also known as Poker decks.

Suits

Sets that a deck of cards is divided into; in poker decks there are four suits of hearts, diamonds, clubs and spades (adopted from French design) and in Tarot the suits are typically seen as water, earth, air, and fire. However, different decks may have different names for the suits

Tarrochi, Tarokk, Taroc

A trick-taking card game played with Tarot decks that may have originated in Renaissance Italy but spread throughout Europe. At some point the decks were used for divinatory purposes and the history of cards splits into that of games and occult purposes with decks taking on many different versions and depictions. Many believe the word Tarot is derived from this.

Tarot

Fortune-telling cards; a system of fortune-telling using (typically) a pack of seventy-eight cards consisting of four suits of fourteen cards (Minor Arcana pips and courts) together with twenty-two picture cards (Major Arcana).

Tarot de Marseilles

Also Tarot of Marseilles; the most popular deck of French origin and dating back to the 15th century.

The suits are the same as the Rider-Waite decks only given in their French terms of "*Bâtons* (Rods, Staves, Scepters, or Wands), *Épées* (Swords), *Coupes* (Cups), and *Deniers* (Coins)."

The court cards in the Minor Arcana are "*Valet* (Knave or Page), *Chevalier* or *Cavalier* (Horse-rider or Knight), *Dame* (Queen) and *Roi* (King)."

The Major Arcana cards are the same as Rider-Waite with the only exceptions being the Tower card called "The House of God" (La Maison Dieu).

The Fool has no number and the Death card has no name but is typically referred to either La Mort (death) or "L'Arcane sans nom" (the card with no name).

The imagery is less detailed then Rider-Waite but are patterned the same and are more reminiscent of the style of the Jack, Queen, King and joker cards we see in playing cards in the US

Trump or Triumph

Terms used to describe a set of cards or suits elevated above the status and rank of other cards in trick-taking card games. In Tarot the trumps are known as the Major Arcana but this is an occult deck phrase only and Major Arcana is not used for trumps used in games. Trump is also a game in which Tarot-like decks were used.

Uprights

cards that used in their upright, or natural, position.

Wild Cards

Bonus cards that add something to the meaning of a reading, generally they fall out when shuffling or putting a deck away.

BIBLIOGRAPHY

(n.d). <u>25 Most Common Symbols.</u> In *School of Metaphysics.* Retrieved on August 16th, 2013 from www.som.org/1dreams/symbols.htm

(6 October 2011). <u>A Witchy Life.</u> In a personal blog. Retrieved on January 6th, 2014 from awitchylife.wordpress.com/2001/10/06/oracle-cards

Abraham, Sylvia. (1998). *How to Use Tarot Spreads.* Minnesota: Llewellyn Publications.

Airey, Raje & Greenwood, Susan. (2006). *The Complete Illustrated Encyclopedia of Witchcraft & Practical Magic.* England: Hermes House Press

Alexander, Skye. (2008). *The Only Tarot Book You Will Ever Need.* Ohio: Adams Media.

Barnett, Lucy. (n.d). <u>The Tarot Dictionary.</u> In *Discover the Meaning of*

Tarot. Retrieved on July 10th, 2012 from www.discover-the-meaning-of-tarot.com/.

(n.d.). Client Bill of Rights. In *Tarot Certification Board of America.* Retrieved on December 21, 2010 from www.tarotcertification.org/rights/html

Calantirniel. (2011) Dowsing for Custom Tarot Spells. In *Llewellyn's Magical Almanac* (p. 134-139). Minnesota: Llewellyn Publications.

Cehovet, Bonnie. (n.d.). *How to Read Tarot Cards.* Retrieved from www.aeclectic.com/Tarot/ ebooks/free.shtml (a free eBook).

Ganly, Sarah; Yahoo Contributor. (29 September 2010). Halloween Party Games and Activities for Adults. In *"Yahoo Voices!"* Retrieved on May 29th, 2012 from voices.yahoo.com/halloween-party-games-activities-6837476.html

Gilbert, John Ph.D. (n.d.). How to Clear Your Tarot Deck of All Negativity. In *The Tarot Institute.* Retrieved on September 29, 2010 from tarotinstitute.com/articles/clear.html

Huggens, Kim. (n.d.). *Tarot 101.* [online course] Retrieved from www.witchschool. com/ page/divinatory-arts

Kenner, Corrine. (2009). *Tarot for Writers.* Minnesota: Llewellyn

Publications.

(n.d). Know Your Tarot. In *Know Your Tarot*. Retrieved on July 10, 2012 from www.knowyourtarot.com/index.html

Lawrence, Baloti D. (1992). *Tarot: 22 Steps to a Higher Path*. London: Meadow Press.

(n.d). Magical Number Correspondences. From *The Wiccan Way*. Retrieved on July 13th, 2013 from www.thewiccanway.org

Renne, Janina. (2000). *Tarot Spells*. Minnesota: Llewellyn Publications.

Reynolds, Lynn; Yahoo Contributor. (8 March 2007). How to Find Your Significator Card in a Tarot Deck. In *"Yahoo Voices!"* Retrieved June 14, 2012 from voices.yahoo.com/how-find-significator-card-tarot-deck-231471.html

Shapiro, Stephen. (9 July 2010). From Tarot Cards to Poker Cards to Personality Poker. In *Stephen Shapiro's 24/7 Innovation*. Retrieved on September 13, 2012 from www.steveshapiro.com /2010/07/09/history-of-poker/

Stenudd, Stefan. (n.d). Tarot Celtic Cross. From *Tarot Meanings and*

Readings. Retrieved on July 13th, 2013 from www.tarotmeaning.org/tarot-celtic-cross.htm

(n.d). Symbolism of Heraldic Elements. In *Fleur de Lis Designs.* Retrieved on August 16th, 2013 from www.fleurdelis.com/meanings.htm

(n.d). Various Articles. In *The Magickal Cat.* Retrieved on January 6th, 2014 from www.themagickalcat.com

Various Authors/Articles. (n.d.) In *Wikipedia, the Free Encyclopedia.* Retrieved on various dates from www.wikipedia.com

Wigington, Patti; About.com Guide. (n.d). *Tarot 101: A Basic Overview.* In *About.Com: Paganism/Wicca.* Retrieved on September 13th, 2012 from paganwiccan.about.com/ od/tarot/p/Intro.htm

Wigington, Patti; About.com Guide. (n.d). *Tarot Inspired Craft Projects.* In *About.Com: Paganism/Wicca.* Retrieved on September 13th, 2012 from Paganwiccan.about.com/od/ tarot/tp/Tarot-Inspired-Craft-Projects.htm

AUTHOR BIO

Deanna has several titles published—among them are two Pagan/Alternative Spirituality titles, "Magick for the Kitchen Witch" and "Magick for the Elemental Witch" which are currently out-of-print but will be re-released this  year. She currently working on two other Pagan books "Magick for the Homesteading Witch" and "Magick for the Wild Witch."

She also writes articles for the online venues of Helium.com and Yahoo Voices! as her local newspaper and two other print venues: *Lakeside Magazine* and *Circle Sanctuary Magazine.*

When she is not writing she enjoys hiking, camping, spending time with her husband and two daughters, and taking picture of wildflowers. She has been practicing Tarot and Paganism for eight years and co-owns a Pagan group in her hometown. You can visit her website andersondeanna.weebly.com and from there you can find links to her at Facebook, Twitter, Amazon and Good Reads.

Made in the USA
San Bernardino, CA
30 July 2014